Chain Chain Change

For Black Women in Abusive Relationships

Expanded second edition

Evelyn C. White

Seal Press

Published by Seal Press
An Imprint of Avalon Publishing Group Incorporated
161 William Street, 16th Floor
New York, NY 10038

Cover and text design by Clare Conrad

Grateful acknowledgment is made to the following for permission to reprint their previously published material:

Lyrics excerpted from "I Never Loved A Man (The Way I Love You)," words and music by Ronnie Shannon. Copyright © Pronto Music & 14th Hour Music. Reprinted by permission. All rights reserved.

Excerpt from "Weekend Glory" from *Shaker, Why Don't You Sing?* by Maya Angelou. Copyright © 1983 by Maya Angelou. Reprinted by permission of Random House, Inc.

Excerpt from *For Colored Girls Who Have Considered Suicide When the Rainbow is Enuf* by Ntozake Shange. Copyright © 1975, 1976, 1977 by Ntozake Shange. Reprinted by permission of Macmillan Publishing Company.

Excerpt from *Movement in Black*. Copyright © 1978 by Pat Parker. Reprinted by permission of The Crossing Press.

Library of Congress Cataloging-in-Publication Data
White, Evelyn C., 1954–
Chain Chain Change : for black women in abusive relationships / Evelyn C. White. — Expanded second edition.
Includes bibliographical references.
1. Wife abuse—United States. 2. Family violence—United States. 3. Afro-American women—Abuse of. 4. Afro-American lesbians—Abuse of. I. Title.
HV6626.W28 1994 362.82'92'08996073—dc20 94-38327
ISBN: 1-878067-60-5

Printed in the United States of America
Expanded second edition, first printing, February 1995
10 9 8 7 6 5

Distributed to the trade by Publishers Group West
In Canada: Publishers Group West Canada, Toronto, Ontario
In the U.K. and Europe: Airlift Book Company, London, England

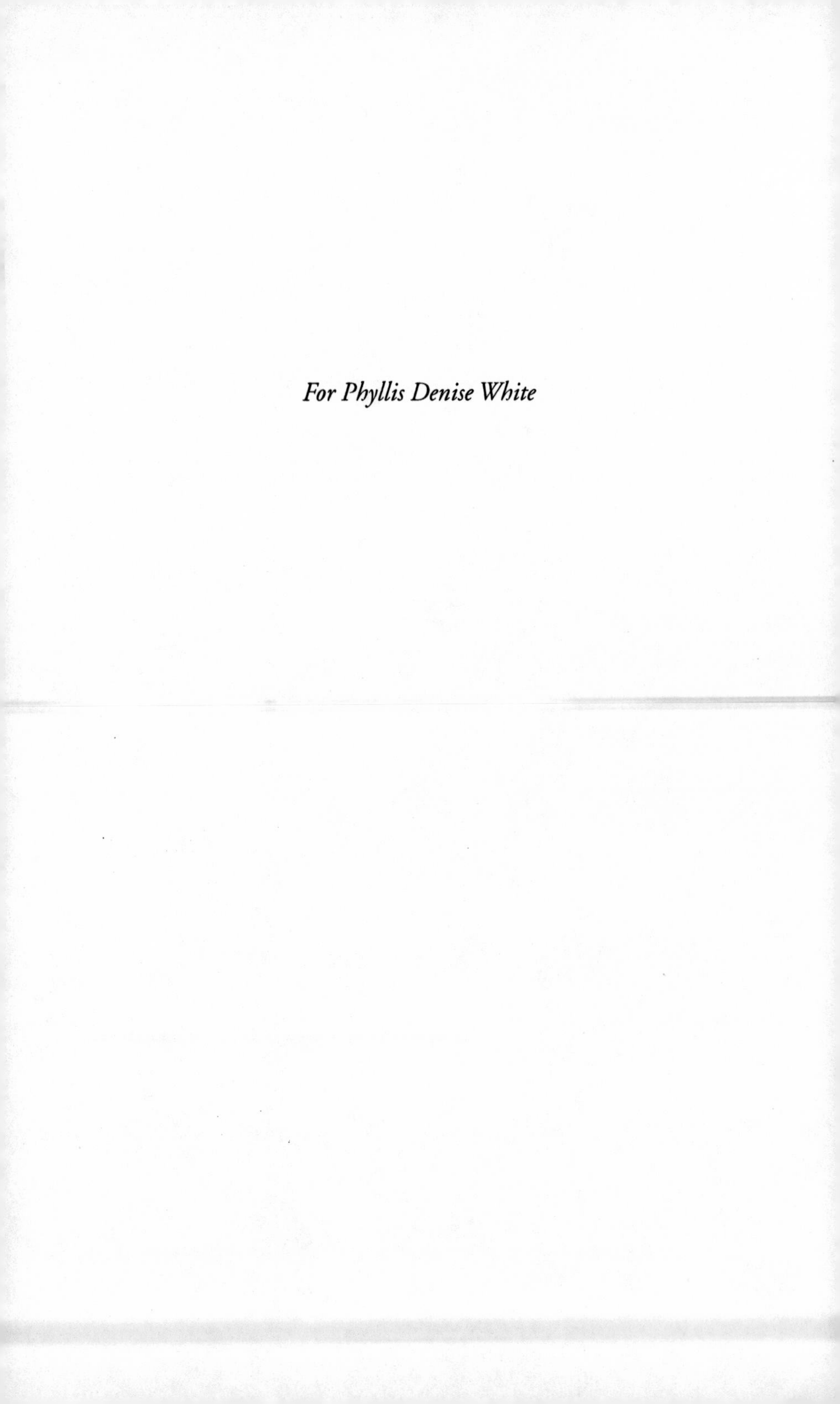

For Phyllis Denise White

Contents

I am a woman with keys
And all the doors are nailed
Dented shut with hammers
Unlikely to ever open on their own
But I am a key woman
I come jingling

— Nikky Finney

Introduction

Ten years after the initial publication of this book, I am able to write, with less anguish, about a matter I could barely mention in the first edition.

My beloved childhood friend Deidra Lynette Henry was stabbed to death at age twenty-one by her husband. In the blind rage that swept over him that bleak December morning, he also killed their three-month-old son and severely injured their two-year-old, sentencing the dimpled, curly-haired toddler to a wheelchair for the rest of his life.

Away at college at the time, I was spared this horrific news until nearly two weeks after Deidra's death. Because Deidra's mother knew I was studying for end-of-semester exams and didn't want to upset me, she asked my family not to tell me about the tragedy. They agreed. Thus, when I arrived home for the holiday break, I was immediately met at the front door by my ten-year-old sister, Phyllis. Knowing the weight of the words she carried and unable to contain herself any longer, she hurriedly blurted out: "Wayne killed Lynette. Didn't nobody want to tell you."

I stood stunned with my bags at my feet, my knee holding the door ajar as the icy winter chill moved through my body. A veil of grief descended over me that still exists.

Although I was dumbstruck by my sister's revelation, I was not completely surprised. It was common knowledge in our neighborhood that Deidra had married a troubled, potentially violent man. In fact, a few months before her death, one sweltering afternoon during my summer vacation, Deidra had stopped by my house for a visit. The paths of our lives had diverged — hers to marriage and motherhood, mine to college and the emerging feminist movement. Still, the bonds we'd developed jumping double-dutch, playing sandlot baseball and giggling over boys at birthday parties remained strong. During our visit, Deidra spoke haltingly about the strains in her marriage as I listened in silence. We were sprawled out on the floor, in my blue bedroom where we'd practiced the clarinet and struggled with algebra. As she was about to leave, Deidra looked me directly in the eye and uttered, as so many battered women do, words designed to mask her terror: "Everybody says he's crazy, but I'm not afraid."

I never saw her again.

Deidra was among the more than 2,000 women killed each year by their intimate partner, according to the U.S. Department of Justice.[1]

The grisly June 1994 slayings of Nicole Brown Simpson and Ronald Goldman — allegedly at the hands of her estranged husband, football legend O. J. Simpson — put a much needed spotlight on the prevalence of battering in American society.*

The Simpson case highlighted, as experts have always maintained, that domestic violence rages among people of all races, religions and socioeconomic backgrounds. No community is immune.

To be sure, public awareness about family violence has increased in the decade since the first edition of this book was published. Police have been trained to better handle domestic calls. Some states require prosecutors and judges to attend workshops on battering as part of their ongoing judicial education. In the recently passed federal crime bill, nearly two billion dollars was allocated to finance the Violence Against Women Act, a law to combat domestic violence. The bill will boost funding for police, prosecutors, battered women's shelters and victim advocates. It will provide for rape education and the creation of a national hotline for abused women.

Despite these advances, battering remains the primary cause of death and injury among women.[2] For African-American women, who experience both race and gender oppression, domestic vio-

---

* The outcome of this case is still pending as this book goes to press.

lence is an especially complex and multilayered demon. As Byllye Y. Avery, founding president of The National Black Women's Health Project, notes:

> When sisters take their shoes off and start talking about what's happening, the first thing we cry about is violence — battering and sexual abuse. The number one issue for most of our sisters is violence. Same thing for their daughters, whether they are twelve or four. We have to look at how violence is used, how violence and sexism go hand in hand. We have to stop it because violence is the training ground for us.[3]

The widespread physical and emotional abuse that Black women suffer rides on an equally immense swell of silence and denial. For example, when University of Oklahoma law professor Anita Hill spoke out about the crude obscenities and unwanted sexual attention that had been directed toward her by now Supreme Court Justice Clarence Thomas, she was openly berated and branded a "traitor" to the race by many African-Americans, both male and female. The sexism that continues to undermine health and healing in the Black community loomed large in a comment heard throughout the Thomas-Hill hearings: "Why would he jeopardize his career over *her?* She's not even worth it." From street corners to mahogany-filled Senate chambers, such anti-Black female sentiments are increasingly being given wide expression in society.

Both actress Robin Givens and beauty pageant contestant Desiree Washington were subject to derision when the women revealed the vicious attacks they'd suffered at the hands of former heavyweight boxing champion Mike Tyson.

Reputedly traumatized by the rape trial during which her morals were presented in an unsavory light, Washington continues to try to heal from her ordeal with "Iron Mike." Tyson, who was sentenced to six years in prison, has been unsuccessful in several attempts to get his conviction overturned.

In the book, *Fire and Fear,* Tyson regales author Jose Torres with details about his ill-fated marriage to Robin Givens:

"Man, I'll never forget that punch. It was when I fought with Robin in Steve's apartment. She really offended me and I went bam," he said, throwing a fast backhand into the air to illustrate. "She flew backward, hitting every fucking wall in the apartment. That was the best punch I've ever thrown in my whole fucking life."[4]

And yet it was Givens who was taunted and accused of being a "golddigger" when she filed for divorce from Tyson. In a 1994 article of *Playboy,* Givens writes of an encounter she had while en route to a movie with her mother: "As we left the car and headed toward the theater, a young woman shouted at me, 'You deserve to get your ass kicked. He should have killed you.'"[5]

Rap music is another arena in which a barrage of violent language and sexist attitudes is being unleashed upon Black women. An emerging musical form when this book was first released, rap is today a multimillion dollar industry that offers the beating, raping and murdering of Black women as major themes.

In "Ain't No Fun (If the Homies Can't Have None)," famed rapper Snoop Doggy Dogg uses a funky beat to sanction gang rape. A widely popular music video crafted by Dr. Dre features a young Black woman whose bikini top is yanked off while she is playing volleyball. In "No Head, No Backstage Pass," the rap group FU2 details the violent sexual assault of an underage female groupie, with rhythmic refrains about sticking safety pins through her nipples.

Commenting about the vulgar, "gangsta" attitudes many rappers express about African-American women, Bushwick Bill (Richard Shaw) of the rap group Geto Boys said: "I call women 'bitches' and 'hos' (whores) because all the women I've met out here are bitches and hos."[6]

The destructive and degrading elements of rap music have rightly drawn the attention of some of the most influential voices in the Black community. "Misogynous rap gives people a false sense of agency," notes cultural critic bell hooks. "It's like we have consumed the worst stereotypes white people have put on Black people."[7]

Indeed, the lyrics of many rap songs promote sexual aggression, woman hatred and remorseless violence in the African-American community. They stoke and fuel behavior we can ill afford in a racist society that already has a stranglehold on our collective necks.

In this new and expanded edition of *Chain Chain Change,* both heterosexual and lesbian Black women will find descriptions of abusive behavior that can help us identify and avoid unhealthy relationships. The book's title is a variation of the soulful "chain chain chain" refrain from Aretha Franklin's hit song "Chain of Fools" and was chosen to convey the message that African-American women can break the cycle of violence that exists in so many of our lives.

Here, you'll read about the specific challenges Black women face in a society that is racist, sexist and homophobic. You'll learn about the images and expectations that erode our self-esteem and keep us feeling like "the mule of the world," regardless of our achievements. Because silence will not protect us, the importance of talking openly about domestic violence and other problems in the Black community is emphasized. That process may not be easy, but it is the only way to work toward positive change.

There is also a chapter about the effects of domestic violence on our children. Understanding the potential risks to children and the harmful messages they receive in a violent household can motivate you to leave an abusive partner.

Subsequent chapters show how the police, health professionals, attorneys, therapists, friends, family members, shelters and the church can help you end the violence in your life. Although the social forces that support domestic violence remain strong, a wide range of resources is available to battered women and many people are working to keep you from hurt and harm. Throughout these chapters you'll read the words of other abused Black women who thought they simply had to take it, perhaps like you do now. While their names have been changed to protect their privacy, all the experiences sisters share in this book are true. Use them as role models who can help you better understand and free yourself from the cycle of violence.

In Chapter Eight, a new addition to this book, one such woman, a formerly battered Black lesbian, shares her story, offering support and guidance for sisters who are being physically and emotionally violated by other women.

In the final chapter, you'll again hear a truth that has been repeated throughout the book: *You deserve and can have a healthy, caring relationship*. You'll be encouraged to seek help from others, but also to realize that you are the best resource for making your life free from abuse. You can learn to love your strengths, accept your weaknesses and embrace life as a flesh and blood human, not the stereotypical strong Black woman.

This book is offered to you, the abused Black woman who wants to change her life. It is also for individuals in the legal, law enforcement, medical, religious, educational and social service professions who attempt to assist you. Please use this book — as has been done with "What's Love Got to Do with It," the much-praised film about Tina Turner — to spread the word that battered Black women *do* rise victorious from physical and emotional abuse.

As much as it pains me, I know this book will not resurrect the bright-eyed Black girl with whom I spent my childhood years. It cannot bring back Deidra's innocence or the dreams for a future she didn't live long enough to realize. This book is too late to save the loving spirit of one Black woman, but I hope it comes in time to protect the preciousness of many others.

Walk in the light.

Evelyn C. White
July 1994
McKenzie River, Oregon

*How to Tell if You Are in an Abusive Relationship**

If you answer yes to one or more of the following questions, you may be experiencing domestic abuse:

- Does your partner constantly criticize you, blame you for things that are not your fault or verbally degrade you?

- Has your partner ever pushed, slapped, kicked, bitten, restrained, thrown objects at or used a weapon against you because he or she was angry or upset?

- Is your partner suspicious and jealous of you? Does he or she make it difficult for you to see friends and family, irrationally accuse you of having affairs or monitor your mail and phone calls?

- Does your partner prevent you from getting or maintaining a job, control your shared resources or restrict your access to money?

- Has your partner forced you to have sex or caused you pain sexually without your consent?

- Has your partner ever threatened to harm you, your family, friends, children, pets or property?

- Has your partner threatened to blackmail you if you leave?

- Does your partner have a history of violence against former partners?

---

* Community United Against Violence, 973 Market Street, Suite 500, San Francisco, California, 94103.

CHAPTER ONE

What Is Domestic Violence?

You're no good heartbreaker, you're a liar and you're a cheat.
And I don't know why I let you do these things to me.
— Aretha Franklin

Who you callin' a bitch? — Queen Latifah

There is a thirty year span between the arrival of Aretha Franklin, Queen of Soul, and rapper Queen Latifah on the heights of the American musical landscape. Yet in their respective songs "I Never Loved a Man (The Way I Love You)" and "U.N.I.T.Y." the acclaimed artists voice a similar concern about the hurt and heartache many Black women suffer in love. Our intimate relationships can often be very complex and confusing, making it difficult for us to identify, understand or stop the abuse we may experience in our daily lives. If any of the questions on the previous page hit home, you are probably being abused.

But have faith. As Aretha and Latifah have done with their music, you are taking positive action by reading this book.

The terms abuse, battering and domestic violence will be used throughout this book. For the most part, they can be used interchangeably to describe your involvement with a partner* who hurts

* You may not be legally married to the person who is abusing you. In this book the term "partner" will be used in reference to both married and unmarried couples. Lesbians involved in abusive relationships will find useful information throughout the book and a discussion of your specific issues and concerns in Chapter 8.

you physically or emotionally. However, there are some subtle differences in their meanings that can help you better understand exactly what is happening to you. This awareness can help you feel less confused and better prepared to explain your experiences when you seek assistance from the police, family members, shelter workers, counselors, attorneys, etc.

Battering means punching, hitting, striking — the actual physical act of one person beating another.

Abuse may include physical assault, but also covers a wide range of hurtful behavior, such as threats, insulting talk, sexual coercion and property destruction.

Domestic violence is a general term used to describe the battering or abusive acts within an intimate relationship. For example, a shelter worker, legal advocate or counselor who helps battered women might say that she or he works in the field of domestic violence.

Physical abuse, emotional abuse and sexual abuse are all forms of domestic violence. Some forms of abuse are serious offenses that can be prosecuted; others are simply behavior that no one should have to put up with. Your partner has no more right to hit you, threaten you or destroy your personal possessions than does a stranger on the streets.

Physical Abuse

You may be wondering if your partner's shove or occasional slap really deserves to be called physical abuse. Maybe he pulls your hair, twists your arm or puts his hand over your mouth to get your attention. He may shadowbox you into a corner and not allow you to move. Perhaps he chases you around your house and then puts a hold on you until you say or do what he wants. Although his behavior may not seem like such a big deal compared to being punched in the face, kicked in the stomach or cut with a knife, these "playful" actions can progress to more serious injuries. Physical abuse often begins with seemingly minor "love taps" or harmless "roughhousing." This behavior can eventually lead to cuts, abrasions, sprained backs, punctured eardrums, black eyes, broken bones and dislocated jaws. Women who are physically abused by their partners may suffer crippling, blindness, miscarriage, loss of consciousness and death. Many domestic disputes become murder statistics every year: Some men actually do beat their partners to death; some women do fight back and perhaps shoot, stab, poison or set fire to the man who is abusing them. While a playful push or punch may seem harmless, your partner's behavior may eventually become more violent. **There is no excuse and no acceptable reason for your partner to ever be physically abusive to you.**

Emotional Abuse

It is possible to be hurt in a relationship even when there is no physical violence. Emotional abuse can be as damaging as a punch in the mouth or a slap in the face. Where there is emotional abuse, there is always the threat of physical assault.

The effects of emotional abuse often last longer than those of physical abuse. As Beverly said, "The bruises from his slaps would eventually heal and go away, but I'll never never forget the awful things he said about the way I look, the way I cook, how I take care of the kids."

If your partner has been emotionally abusive to you, you are likely to feel depressed, anxious, ashamed and powerless. You may believe that people don't like you. Although you'd like to change your life, you feel trapped in a confusing situation and very insecure. You may believe, as your partner has told you repeatedly, that you are unattractive, worthless, unable to survive on your own and that you bring your misery upon yourself. Worst of all, you may come to believe that all Black men are like your partner and that all Black women suffer as you do in their relationships. The truth is that his constant emotional abuse, in addition perhaps to physical abuse, has worn you down and caused you to feel bad about yourself. **You do not deserve to be emotionally abused by your partner. You have a right to a considerate and caring relationship.**

Sexual Abuse

Sexual matters can be very difficult and embarrassing to talk about. You may consider reporting physical abuse, emotional abuse or property destruction, but never dream of telling anyone that your partner's sexual interactions with you are unpleasant, frightening or violent. Because of your attitudes about marriage or your general views about female sexuality, you may believe it is your duty to perform any sexual act your partner desires, even though you don't find it pleasurable.

Your partner may reinforce these feelings by telling you that your attitudes about sex are old-fashioned or that other women will participate in the sexual activities that you won't. If you decide to seek professional help about this problem, you may be told that no sexual act between consenting adults is "wrong" or be misunderstood because of stereotypes about the sexual behavior of Black women.

Yet it is very important for you to control your body and express yourself freely in sex, the most intimate and vulnerable of acts. For if you feel demeaned, disrespected or violated in your sexual interactions, those negative feelings are very likely to influence how you feel about other aspects of your life. **You don't have to submit to sexual acts you don't like. You deserve warm and nurturing sexual experiences with your partner.**

Destructive Acts

Some men display their violent behavior by destroying objects or pets. These destructive acts may be their only demonstration of abusive behavior, or they might also engage in other, already described forms of abuse.

If you woke up one morning and discovered that someone had smashed all the windows in your car, you would no doubt report it to the police. You'd probably feel you had been the victim of a destructive, criminal act.

If your partner damages your car or your house or kills your pet, he is committing the same type of crime as the stranger who smashed your car windows. If he intentionally damages items that belong to you as a form of punishment, he is abusing you. He may say, "Look at what you made me do," after destroying a gift he has given you, but you are not responsible for his behavior. **You do not deserve, nor do you have to be the victim of, destructive acts by your partner.**

Domestic Violence — Hurtful Words and Actions

Your feelings of shame and fear and your isolation from other abused women may cause you to believe that every woman has a loving and nurturing partner except you. In fact, the abuse of women has been accepted throughout history and exists in all societies. In every major culture of the world there has been and is legal and cultural support for words and actions that keep women physically, emotionally and economically subordinate to men.

Although it was romanticized as a symbol of gentility, the ancient Chinese practice of binding women's feet is best understood by the old Chinese proverb: "Feet are bound, not to make them beautiful as a curved bow, but to restrain women when they go outdoors."

Menstruation, clearly one of the most natural and organic symbols of womanhood, has been considered taboo and unclean among many peoples of the world. Early Hindus believed that, "The wisdom, the energy, the strength, the right and the vitality of a man utterly perish when he approaches a menstruating woman."

Among the Fanti people of Ghana, if a woman was disowned by her family, her children were too because "children follow the mother's condition." However, if a man was disowned, his status alone was affected.[1]

Like these cultural traditions, the physical abuse of women has been taken for granted universally as part of the natural order of male dominance over women. The Russians said: "A wife may love a husband who never beats her, but she does not respect him." The Spanish: "Never hit your woman with the petal of the rose but with the thorny stem." The English: "A woman, a horse and a hickory tree, the more you beat 'em, the better they be."

Times have changed, but the underlying message of these proverbs still holds true today. A glance at any newspaper or television broadcast will confirm that violence, and especially violence against women, is widespread and accepted in the United States today. Most "action" shows on TV show men fighting with each other, but in fact it is women and children who are the most frequent targets of male violence. Authorities estimate that every hour, as many as 70 women across the country will be attacked by rapists.[2] This violence is a means of control and is also directed against the poor, the elderly and the disabled. Violence against minorities also has a long history in this culture and continues today. Witness the infamous beating of motorist Rodney King at the hands of the Los Angeles police.

Because violence surrounds us outside the home, many people find it easy to accept it in the home as well. Teachers, social workers, police, the courts, ministers, doctors and neighbors have contributed, through their silence, to the systematic denial of the existence and severity of domestic violence. Although abused women come from all races, religions, classes and occupations, there is a tendency to label battering a class or race problem, and to claim that it only happens to other people. Yet FBI statistics indicate that a woman is beaten every eighteen seconds in this country and that twenty-eight percent of female victims of murder are slain by husbands or boyfriends.[3] Physical punishment continues to be used to keep women in their place — whether that woman is the wealthy businessman's wife who hides in the Mercedes every Saturday night to avoid being beaten or the junior high school girl who is just starting to date a possessive older boy.

◆

The Impact of Sex Roles

Rigidly defined sex roles, combined with historical traditions that oppress women, contribute to the social acceptance of battering. For instance, aggression, competitiveness, power, strength and stoicism are widely considered to be hallmarks of a healthy, mature male.

These attitudes are reinforced by sayings like, "it's a man's world" and "that's a man's job," which are repeated over and over through generations and which, indeed, men are expected to live up to. For in this culture, educational, political, religious, recreational and military institutions all support and provide role models for masculinity that are aggressive and authoritative. Men are expected and encouraged to assert themselves with brute force if need be.

Even after the changes brought about by the women's movement, these attitudes and expectations about masculinity remain very strong. Rare is the parent (probably yourself included) who really expects a male child to wash dishes or vacuum or who encourages him to pursue a career as a nurse or librarian, because those are considered "women's jobs" (and therefore have lower status and lower pay). Equally rare is the parent who really expects a female child to take out the garbage or mow the lawn or to study physics and become an aerospace engineer. As girls, and then as women, we are expected to be submissive, dependent, passive, indecisive, weak and emotional in this society.

As a result of this strict sex-role stereotyping, both men and women are constrained when they attempt to express their full range of emotions and abilities. A woman who demonstrates too many "masculine" characteristics is very likely to be called unfeminine or headstrong or a lesbian. A man who speaks softly or interacts with others unaggressively may be called effeminate or weak. If he enjoys or pursues a career in fashion, opera, music or dance, he may be presumed homosexual because those professions emphasize grace, beauty and sensitivity.

It is almost impossible for men or women to live up to society's demanding requirements of them. Men cannot always be "manly," nor can women always be "ladylike." The pressure to conform to sex roles takes its toll on all of us. Most men, for instance, have not been taught how to express their "feminine" emotions. On the contrary, they have been told that they should never cry and that they should always fight back when challenged. They have not been allowed to express the helplessness, vulnerabilities, fears, feelings of pain and insecurity that all humans feel at some time. This inability to say "I hurt" or "I'm frightened" causes some men to cover up their vulnerabilities by carrying out the masculine role to the extreme. Without permission or models to express insecurity, dependency or low self-esteem, some men kick instead of crying. Gloria, an African-American woman who married the captain of her high school football team, illustrates the point with these comments about her abusive partner:

> I think basically he does love the family, loves the children and cares about me. But he is so afraid of being judged by others. When he feels that his mother or the neighbors think he is not a good provider, it causes him great dissatisfaction. He may say he doesn't care what people think, but he looks for approval from everybody. I think it's because he never felt good enough as a child.

The particular circumstances that prompt their violence may vary; however, many abusive men tend to be controlled and conflicted by the sex role society expects them to fulfill. Although they may appear to be "tough guys," many are often insecure, emotionally dependent, vulnerable and unable to deal with stress in a healthy or productive way.

How Does Battering Start and Continue?

Battering can begin at any time during a relationship and continue throughout it. It can happen on your first date, on your wedding night, after you get a job, after sad times or happy ones.

Some abused women report that the violence begins shortly

after they tell their partner they are pregnant and that the abuse continues while they are carrying the child. They say that their partner often accuses them of having sex with other men and demands proof that he is the father of the child. The violence may be related to the man's jealousy or dependence on the woman. He may be upset that he must begin to share her with a child. Or perhaps he wants her to terminate the pregnancy and spare him the pressures and responsibilities of providing for a child. Because many abusive men hold traditional, conservative views, violence that results in miscarriage may be more acceptable to them than abortion.

Your pregnancy can be one of the many excuses your partner may use to rationalize his behavior against you. He may try to blame the behavior on his alcohol or drug abuse. Statistics do show that many men are under the influence of alcohol or drugs when they become violent, but these substances do not cause the abuse. Abusive men who have successfully completed alcohol or drug treatment programs still batter, and some alcoholics/addicts never batter. It is not the substance that causes battering.

The "Cycle of Violence"

In her groundbreaking book *The Battered Woman,* Dr. Lenore Walker describes the cyclical pattern of battering.[4] An awareness of this cycle can help you understand that you are not the cause of your partner's abuse and that you cannot change it. His abusive behavior is something only he can change or learn how to control.

Tension-building is the first stage of the cycle. During this stage the man is irritable, uncommunicative and quick-tempered. He may claim to be upset about his job and have a short attention span. He breaks dishes, throws objects, has shouting fits, but then quickly apologizes. It is during this period that an abused woman may report feeling as though she were walking on eggs. She does everything she can to pacify or amuse her partner in hopes of preventing his violent outburst.

The tension increases and eventually rises, in the second stage of the cycle, to a physical or verbal explosion. A disagreement, traffic ticket, late meal or misplaced car keys may send the batterer into a violent rage, and he chooses to vent his anger and frustration by assaulting the person he is closest to. During this stage, an abused woman may be beaten for seemingly minor reasons or no apparent reason at all. It is not uncommon for the batterer to wake his partner from a sound sleep and begin an onslaught of verbal or physical abuse. For instance, Cheyenna had this to say, "At two o'clock in the morning he woke me up and demanded that I help him clean out the aquarium. I refused, and he broke my nose."

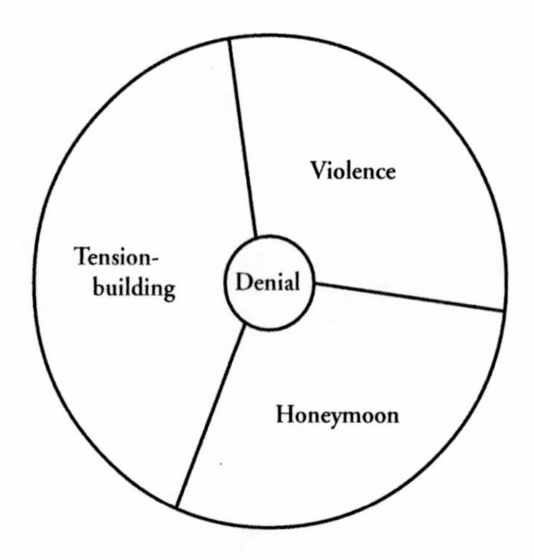

Dr. Walker calls the third stage of the cycle the "honeymoon phase." The batterer becomes extremely loving, kind and apologetic for his abusive behavior. He seems to be remorseful and genuinely sorry that he has hurt the woman he loves. He makes promises to stop drinking, using drugs, gambling, worrying about his job, seeing other women, visiting his mother, hanging out with his friends, or whatever it is he believes is causing him to behave violently. The abused woman believes these promises because she doesn't want to be beaten again or lose what now appears to be a very caring partner and nurturing relationship. It is during this stage, when her partner brings her flowers, buys her gifts, takes her out to dinner and spends extra time with the children, that the abused woman's dreams of love and romance are fulfilled. She believes that her household has been magically transformed into the classic happy family, and that the two previous stages of the cycle will never happen again.

In reality, like the moon, the "honeymoon phase" wanes. The abused woman finds herself tiptoeing delicately around her partner as the tension-building stage starts again.

New Attitudes

The recognition of domestic violence as a deeply-rooted problem in our society has come from several sources, most notably the women's movement. Anti-rape organizers of the early 1970s first showed how women have been historically blamed for the brutal and violent crime of rape, and then silenced because of guilt and shame. Grassroots activists and, increasingly, social service professionals borrowed organizing and counseling techniques from the rape crisis movement to illustrate and address the similar plight of battered women. As public consciousness about sexism and its violent impact on all women's lives began to grow, shelters for battered women opened and social and legal reforms began to take place. With the anthem, "We will not be beaten," abused women and their supporters organized across the country.

Although it continues to face many cultural and economic challenges, the battered women's movement is here to stay. As an abused woman, you need not be silent or feel ashamed about the violence in your life any longer. There are many people working to change the forces that make your partner feel he has a right to hit you, as well as to change a society that supports violence of all kinds.

Being able to identify and understand (not accept) the physical, emotional or sexual abuse or destructive acts you suffer can help you feel less confused or responsible for your partner's behavior. It's not anything you've done, but rather sexist traditions and attitudes that perpetuate violence against women and children.

You may be thinking, "This is true for white people, but Black views and experiences are different." You are right. As an abused Black woman, you must deal with the effects of both woman-hatred and racial discrimination in our society. In the next chapter you'll find out how you have been helped and harmed by your experiences.

CHAPTER TWO

The Psychology of Abuse

In addition to sexist and racist attitudes within the general society, an abused Black woman has to deal with the complexity of her position within the African-American community. Understanding the special pressures on you and coming to grips with the sources of your joy and pain can put your relationship with an abusive partner in better perspective. This insight can help you to celebrate and protect Black traditions that truly enrich you and to challenge those that contribute to your abuse.

Images and Expectations of Black Women

In 1928, African-American writer and folklorist Zora Neale Hurston wrote an essay, "How It Feels to Be Colored Me." Today, her words are still very much needed to help Black women overcome the destructive images and unrealistic expectations that contribute to our physical and emotional abuse.

> I am not tragically colored. There is no great sorrow lurking behind my eyes. I do not mind at all. I do not belong to the sobbing school of Negrohood who hold that nature somehow has given them a lowdown dirty deal and whose feelings are all hurt about it. Even in the helter-skelter skirmish that is my life, I have seen that the world is to the strong regardless of a little pigmentation more or less. No, I do not weep at the world — I am too busy sharpening my oyster knife.[1]

The image of Black women as long-suffering victims can keep us passive and confused about the abuse in our lives. Not only do we experience these feelings in our intimate relationships, but they impact our daily experiences as well.

In a contemporary parallel to Hurston's essay, noted Black feminist scholar Barbara Smith points out, ". . . it is not something we have done that has heaped this psychic violence and material abuse upon us, but the very fact, that because of who we are, we are multiply oppressed."[2]

And who are we? Abolitionist Harriet Tubman, civil rights activist Fannie Lou Hamer, choreographer Katherine Dunham, playwright Lorraine Hansberry, astronaut Mae Jemison, journalist Charlayne Hunter-Gault, health advocate Dr. Joycelyn Elders, Olympic champion Jackie Joyner-Kersee, and academician Barbara Jordan are all part of our glorious Black female heritage. Yet too often are the images of Black women reduced to the big-bosomed slave "mammy" or the wigged and high-heeled streetwalker with equally stereotypical "evil," "domineering" and "bitchy" images in between.

The often repeated retort that African-American women are honored within our communities is far too simplistic. It does not address the reality of the many hardships that go along with being Black and female. For instance, according to recent research, the national homicide rate for African-American women is 12.3 per 100,000 murders compared to 2.9 for white women; Black women between the age of sixteen and twenty-four are three times as likely to be raped than white women; fifty-seven percent of us raise our children alone; with a weekly median wage of $288, we remain at the bottom of the economic ladder.[3] We have been "honored" to endure these and other burdens that have often kept us from participating fully in life. And we have done so, not because we like being burdened, but because sexist and racist social systems have frequently given us little choice.

The images and expectations of African-American women are actually both *super-* and *sub-*human. This conflict has created myths and stereotypes that cause confusion about our own identity and make us targets for abuse. Like Shug Avery in Alice Walker's *The Color Purple,* Black women are considered wild — but also rigid and "proper." We are unattractive — but exotic, like supermodel Naomi Campbell. We are passive — but rabble-rousing like politician Maxine Waters. We are streetwise — but insipid like Prissy, who "didn't know nothin' about birthin' no babies" in *Gone with the Wind.* We are considered evil, but self-sacrificing; stupid, but conniving; domineering while at the same time obedient to our men; and sexually inhibited, yet promiscuous. Covered by what is considered our seductively rich, but repulsive brown skin, Black women are perceived as inviting but armored. Society finds it difficult to believe that we really need physical or emotional support like all women of all races.

The Tyranny of Color

All Black people have, in fact, been damaged by the impact of color in this culture. A white Christmas or white-collar job are considered good and positive things whereas to be blacklisted, blackmailed or called the "black sheep of the family" have always had negative connotations. Although it may appear unimportant now that we are supposed to have achieved Black pride, these images are constantly affirmed and reinforced within society. They have caused some African-American men, and indeed some Black women, to believe that white people, and therefore white women, are "better" and more desirable than we are. Alice Walker writes in her essay "The Civil Rights Movement: What Good Was It?":

> My mother, a truly great woman who raised eight children of her own and half a dozen of the neighbors' without a single complaint, was convinced that she did not exist compared to "them." She subordinated her soul to theirs and became a faithful and timid supporter of the "Beautiful White People." Once she asked me, in a moment of vicarious pride and despair, if I didn't think "they" were "jest naturally smarter, prettier, better."[4]

Stereotypes about African-American women contribute to the confusion, inferiority and insecurity that you already feel because of the abuse in your life. These negative and often conflicting images may make you wonder who you really are and what is really expected of you from your partner and society.

Talking about these pressures with other African-American women can help you to define your identity and eliminate the many myths and stereotypes about Black women. Make a list of all the Black women you identify with and evaluate the parts of them you see in yourself. Likewise make a list of all the African-American women you do not like and look at what you find unappealing or threatening about them. If you could be any Black woman in the world, who would you choose to be? Think about whether your choice is based on this woman's real contribution to enhancing the [a]image and achievements of African-Americans, or if you'd like to be her because she is accepted by society and longed for by the average Black man.

There are many passionate and celebratory aspects of our lives. Black women are as diverse in our ways of being as the rest of society. But this is easily forgotten, as are many of our heroines, in the face of persistent messages that tell us our hair is too kinky, our behinds too wide and our tempers too quick.

Expressing your feelings about the complexity of your identity and the pain of your relationship is a healthy first step toward making you feel better about who you really are. If you don't feel comfortable talking to other African-American women about these issues, consider keeping a journal where you can write about your feelings and essentially talk to yourself. After exploring all that has kept you feeling down and out, you'll find it much easier to nurture yourself and get in touch with all the things you really love about being a Black woman. Affirming yourself will help you understand and begin to challenge the abuse in your relationship and in your daily experiences. With time, you're likely to find yourself feeling like Maya Angelou in her poem "Weekend Glory":

My life ain't heaven
but it sure ain't hell.
I'm not on top
but I call it swell
if I'm able to work
and get paid right
and have the luck to be Black
on a Saturday night.

The Abused Woman — What's Love Got to Do with It?

Abused women have a tendency to put everyone's needs before their own. Because of our cultural history, this conditioning in African-American women is particularly strong. Perhaps more than others, an abused woman is likely to hold traditional views about love, romance and relationships. You make a commitment to your partner and even if you do not marry, you have a big investment in the relationship. If married, you are likely to believe that your vows are sacred and expect a loving union with your partner for life. In exchange for fulfilling the traditional role of homemaker, you expect your partner to protect and provide for you physically, emotionally and economically. Abused women usually give above and beyond the call of duty to their relationships.

Thus when you are assaulted by the man you love, your beliefs and expectations about your relationship are shattered as well as your body. Many abused women refer to the experience as having the rug pulled out from under their feet. There have probably been many good times in the relationship. Despite their violent behavior, abusive males can be loving toward their children and are sometimes greatly admired within their community. Consequently the abused woman faces conflicts both in her home and in her heart.

The entire nature of the relationship changes when your partner becomes violent. You believe that the violence is your fault — that it happens because you have failed to keep the children quiet or get the dinner on the table as soon as he comes home. Your self-blame is quickly reinforced by your partner, who as a batterer has learned to blame his violent behavior on you, the children, alcohol or job pressures.

In order to get things back on safe footing you are likely to work harder — to cook better meals, to always be ready when he comes to take you out for the evening, to give your partner more attention and to be more "feminine" — sweet, gentle and quiet. But it is your partner who is responsible for his behavior, however much he has conditioned you to believe it is your fault. It is important to realize that no amount of good cooking, love, attention or self-blame on your part will stop an abusive man from striking out when his tension level builds up. Until your partner learns how to deal with stress in a healthy way, he is likely to continue venting his frustrations on you.

It is not your responsibility to placate your partner or understand his excuses for his behavior, but to protect yourself from his violence and anger.

The Abusers

Because of institutionalized and individual racism in American society, Black men, in particular, have experienced much of the powerlessness, low self-esteem, feelings of ineffectiveness and insecurity that characterize many abusive men. In *The Third Life of Grange Copeland*, Alice Walker writes with eloquent, insightful passion about the devastating effects of racism on a Southern Black family. She explains, but by no mean excuses, the violent actions that some African-American men direct toward Black women — the individuals *least* responsible for their suffering.

> His crushed pride, his battered ego, made him drive Mem away from schoolteaching. Her knowledge reflected badly on a husband who could scarcely read and write. It was his great ignorance that sent her into white homes as a domestic, his need to bring her down to his level! It was his rage at himself, and his life and his world that made him beat her for an imagi-

> nary attraction she aroused in other men, crackers, although she was not party to any of it. His rage and his anger and his frustration ruled. His rage could and did blame everything, *everything* on her.[5]

Clearly the experiences of slavery, lynchings, segregation, imprisonment and daily urban living have taken their toll on Black men. Historically viewed by whites as rapists, pimps, drug addicts, superstuds and superathletes, Black men are some of the most maligned members of American society.

Many Black men feel, for good reason, that they have no power and little impact on the culture at large. Thus they are more likely to demand that their partners and family members treat them like a man and show them respect. Any challenge, any question from his partner can be interpreted as yet another attempt to chip away at his already insecure and fragile sense of self. For African-American men know that regardless of how hard they work, most will never become a part of the power structure of American society. And the few who do pay a price for their "success" with increased physical and mental stress.

The early deaths, high unemployment rate and excessive imprisonment of Black men are directly related to racism in this society. In addition, racism has contributed to a statistic with far-reaching implications for relationships between Black women and Black men. According to a recent Census Bureau report, twenty-two percent of Black women age forty to forty-four have never married, compared with seven percent of white women and nine percent of Hispanic women.[6] When one considers the existence of gay Black men and those who choose to be involved with non-Black women, the number of African-American men available for relationships with Black women becomes even less. This situation is very significant in terms of the tensions that exist between Black women and Black men.

The average African-American man frequently struggles to provide his family with basic necessities. He looks for role models in the culture and finds, for the most part, athletes, entertainers, drug addicts, and armed robbers — the extreme successes and failures within society. The Black man may decide that if nothing else, he will at least control what happens in his home and within his family. He may behave abusively because, like most men, he has not learned how to express his pain, frustration, lack of confidence and insecurity about his impotence in the world. But abusing those he loves only serves to make him feel worse, not better, about himself. For he has confirmed the racist stereotype about the violent nature of Black men. He may come to believe that he deserves to be feared as much as society fears him.

The Black Woman's Response

African-American women live in the same racist society that Black men do and therefore cannot help but be sympathetic to what they suffer. We know that the Black family has been damaged by slavery, lynchings and systematized social, economic and educational discrimination. Though we have surely been divided as African-American men and women, our mutual suffering has prevented us from completely turning our backs on each other.

In fact, our acute understanding of the oppression of Black men has forced us to wrestle with a critical question posed by Black activist and religious scholar Maryviolet C. Burns: "What do you do with men of color who menace women of color in a world where people of color are oppressed?"[7]

Black women have been conditioned to repair the damage that has been done to Black families because we feel it is our responsibility to keep the family together at all costs. We have been willing to let our children grow up with imperfect role models because men are scarce in our communities.

The importance of the facade of stability in family life was emphasized very poignantly by fifty-one Black children in Chicago. They took out a newspaper ad begging their absent fathers to show up so they could be loved and honored on Father's Day.[8] In addition to the hardships we will endure for our children, we do not personally wish to give up the tenderness and affection that even abusive men express some of the time. Black women, like all human beings, desire love, attention and protection.

However, because you are sensitive to the effects of racism and the victimization of African-American men, does *not* mean that you should continue to endure abuse from your partner. As the late poet Pat Parker wrote,

> *Brother*
> *I don't want to hear*
> *about*
> *how* my *real enemy*
> *is the system.*
> *i'm no genius,*
> *but i do know*
> *that system*
> *you hit me with*
> *is called*
> *a fist.*

You do not have to become your partner's target because the bank didn't give him a loan. You do not have to become the scapegoat when the landlord raises the rent. And you do not have to become the punching bag because he can't afford to take the children to Disneyland.

Physical and emotional abuse are not acceptable demonstrations of Black manhood, even though your partner, family or friends may try to make excuses for his behavior. Black men will *not* heal their wounded pride or regain a sense of dignity by abusing Black women. It is important for you to hold your partner accountable for every injury he inflicts. By doing so you stop contributing to your own pain as well as to his self-destructiveness.

There are real pressures like poverty and discrimination that have contributed to the disruption of the Black family. But it is not until we begin to address these issues openly and take responsibility for what we can change within our families that we will move beyond our victimized status. For you, as an abused Black woman, this means saying, "No," to the abusive behavior of a partner that threatens you or your children. Taking such action does not mean you want to emasculate him, but that you believe you have a right to a loving relationship. When your partner learns how to treat you with care and understanding, he'll feel better about himself and his abilities.

Changing strong, culturally supported patterns of behavior may be a very long and difficult process for both you and your partner. On your own, you might not be strong enough to spend a special occasion like your birthday without him, even though you know he might become violent. Without some kind of help, he may not be able to take a walk, instead of hitting you, when he has to work extra hours.

Sometimes, the only solution for your self-protection is to leave your partner temporarily or, if need be, permanently.

CHAPTER THREE

Stay or Leave?

The reasons women choose to stay in or leave an abusive relationship are rarely ever clear-cut or simple. Some days you may be absolutely convinced that you will not stay with your partner another minute. Other days you may not be able to imagine a life without him. Living in an abusive situation distorts your views about what exactly the relationship represents to you. Understanding the emotional and practical issues involved in your abuse will help you develop a better strategy for your survival and self-protection, whether you decide to stay or leave.

Why Do You Stay?

In addition to your awareness of the Black man's victimization, you probably stay with or return to your abusive partner out of fear. You know that he will physically harm you if you leave or act independently because he has done so before. He may have isolated you from family and friends so that you feel completely dependent upon him. Or you may have isolated yourself out of fear and shame that someone will discover you are in an abusive relationship and, in the "blame the victim" tradition, judge you a failure. You may want to protect your partner's job (your source of income) or your reputation in your community. You may believe, as he's told you, that you can't live without him, can't find anyone else who would tolerate a "stupid" and "worthless" woman like yourself. You may feel sorry for him because he has a substance abuse problem, was raised in a violent household himself, or because he threatens to commit suicide if you leave. As Myesha said:

> After he'd beaten me, he'd cry. He'd say he was sorry and it was just like he was a little boy. He'd be so scared I was going to leave him. You can't help but feel bad, that it's your fault when you see a big, strong man cry. Sometimes I really believed he'd kill himself if I left.

As an abused woman you may want the relationship you're in, but without the violence.

All of these factors may cause you to behave in ways that others view as crazy, stupid or self-destructive because they don't understand the particular dynamics of the cycle of violence or domestic violence.

You also stay in the relationship because you feel physically, emotionally and financially trapped by society's expectations of you. You know that people think you're crazy for staying in an abusive relationship, but will consider you a failure if you leave. It seems both your fault that you are beaten and your fault that you are too terrified or ashamed to ask for help. Your self-blame may be reinforced by your family, friends, police and clergy, and by legal, medical and mental health professionals who may try to make you feel that you are responsible for your abuse. Because of their lack of sensitivity and understanding of domestic violence they may not support your efforts to stop his violence or to leave the relationship.

Instead of acknowledging your survival skills and enormous ability to cope, society considers you weak and masochistic. As an abused woman, you are denied the compassion, forgiveness and understanding that you characteristically give to everyone but yourself. You feel shamed and disgraced by your experiences. But the disgrace is not yours. It belongs to the society that fails to protect, counsel and console you.

Think About It

Many abused women look at their situation and decide that staying with their abusive partners is better than leaving. Because of the importance placed on having a man in our society, they believe that an abusive relationship is better than no relationship at all. You might also choose to stay in your relationship because you receive financial support from your partner, do not wish to disrupt your children's lives by moving, do not want to disclose the violence to family or friends, want the family to be together when your partner reforms as he promises to do, or you believe that even a violent home is safer and less threatening than the outside world.

Because women are conditioned to make sacrifices and try to work things out, no matter what, you may avoid taking an objective look at the perils of staying in an abusive relationship, some of which can be as plain as the bruises on your body, others perhaps not so obvious. If your partner does not make efforts to change his behavior and you stay in the relationship, chances are that you will continue to suffer violence that may eventually lead to permanent injury or death. You will continue to have low self-esteem, little self-confidence and feel isolated from family members and friends. In order to cope with your daily existence, you may develop a drug or alcohol dependency. Your children will be exposed to violent behavior that may later cause them to become abusive or abused.

What You Can Do If You Stay

If you choose to stay in an abusive relationship, it does not mean that your situation is completely hopeless or that it is not possible to begin to make changes in your life. What it does mean, however, is that you and your children remain more vulnerable to violence that will become more frequent and more severe. Your partner's abusive behavior will not change unless he makes a commitment to changing it.

So if you stay, one of the best things you can do is to start taking measures that will protect you physically and emotionally from his abuse. You can begin to do this by finding out as much as possible about the situation you're choosing to remain in. By reading this book, you are already taking better care of yourself. You can find other books and articles about domestic violence at your local library or bookstore (see Resources). You can also begin to break through feelings of isolation if you talk with trusted friends and family members about the abuse in your life.

Because children often feel they are responsible for the arguments and fighting between their parents, it is very important that you explain (as best you can, given their ages), that they are not the cause of the violence in your household. Explain to them that you are concerned about their safety and are trying to make things better for everyone.

You can begin to develop a safety plan to protect you and your children. Prepare a list of the phone numbers of people you can depend on in an emergency. Get an extra set of keys made for the car. Put away some cash to be used for a taxi or to buy bus tickets. Think about how much emergency clothing you would need for you and your children. Pack a small bag and put it away. If you develop a safety plan in advance, it will be easier to take action when you need to use it.

Although you are still in an abusive relationship you can begin to think about what it would be like to live independently. Imagine how you would earn money, where you would live and what kinds of friends you'd like to have. Find out about classes from a local community college. The Urban League or employment office may have information about job training programs. A church in your area might provide emergency assistance or space for battered women's support groups. Remember you can go to a battered women's support group while still in a relationship (see Chapter 7). Organizations like the National Black Women's Health Project and the YWCA will be able to give you information about shelters, counseling, how to file for divorce, etc.

These are just some of the ways you can begin to think about and take steps toward a life and relationships without violence.

Leaving

Although it means freedom from your partner's violence, making the decision to leave your home can be hard. This is because any change, even a positive one, causes stress. You may feel as though you've failed or get down on yourself for uprooting your children. Even though he's hurt you physically and emotionally many times, you are likely to feel guilty for leaving a man who is insecure, feels inadequate and is dependent on you. As Beth Richie, an expert on domestic violence, writes, a strong sense of racial loyalty also makes it harder for African-American women to leave an abusive relationship.

> Loyalty and devotion are enormous barriers to overcome. Black women be forewarned: there is already so much negative information about our families that a need to protect ourselves keeps us quiet. It is a painful, unsettling task to call attention to violence in our community.[1]

With all these things going through your head, you may lose sight of the real reason you are leaving. You would probably not be putting yourself and your children through such change were there not a very good reason for you to go. No doubt that reason is that you are deathly afraid — for your life. Remember his most violent blow and that there is a possibility you might not survive the next one. Keep in mind that the longer you stay in an abusive relationship, the clearer the message is to your partner that there is nothing wrong with his behavior or that you are "strong" enough to take it.

There are many options to consider after you have decided to leave an abusive relationship. Though the choices may seem very confusing and hard at that moment, you should be proud of yourself for putting the safety of you and your children first.

As you are making the decision to leave, it is also important to note that research shows battered women are most likely to suffer severe or lethal injuries when attempting to report abuse or leave a violent relationship.

Your partner may interpret your leaving as the ultimate assault on his manhood and vent his anger with extreme force and brutality. Unwilling to accept that they no longer control the lives of their ex-wives or former girlfriends, many batterers still lash out long after their relationships have ended.

For example, National Crime survey data shows that in almost seventy-five percent of spouse-on-spouse assaults, the victim was divorced or separated at the time of the incident.[2]

This does not mean that you should stay with an abusive partner. Rather, it underscores the importance of having a well-developed plan of action that attends to your safety should you decide to leave.

Depending on your circumstances and your finances, you might go to a battered women's shelter, or to a motel, friend's house or the home of relatives or friends in other states. Perhaps a former employer or as in Brenda's case, a former school teacher, would be willing to help you.

> I guess I thought about school because of the children, I don't know. Anyway, I knew that my old fifth-grade teacher was still teaching. It was hard, but I went there and told her I needed a place to stay because my husband was beating me. She remembered me and told me I could stay at her house as long as I needed to.

Regardless of where you go or for how long, you should take a packed bag of clothes and important documents such as birth certificates, bank books and medical records with you. Take the money you have stashed away, or withdraw as much from an account as you'll need. You may have to borrow some money from an understanding friend or family member for an indefinite period of time.

If you have not already removed items of real or sentimental value, such as jewelry, family photographs, your children's drawings, your high school yearbook, items your parents have given you, etc., do so before you leave your household. Your partner may destroy anything he thinks is important to you once he discovers you've left. One abused woman reported that she found the recipes she used to prepare her husband's favorite meals torn up and scattered all over the kitchen when she returned with the police to get more clothes.

Remember that it is not cruel, selfish or unfair for you to take what is rightfully yours. You should not feel guilty about taking anything that will insure that you and your children will be safe, clothed and have enough to eat for a while.

Avoid the temptation to tell anyone exactly when or where you're going unless you are absolutely sure that person is committed to your safety. For not only is your partner likely to try to find you through his own means, but he also may badger and harass anyone he thinks has information about you. The best way to prevent a friend or relative from giving in to your partner's demands out of fear or sympathy is to make sure they don't know where you are. When you are settled and secure you can decide with whom you wish to share your whereabouts and future plans.

It's not easy, but it is possible to plan, save money and develop the emotional stamina and confidence to leave your abusive partner. Thousands of abused women have done it. You can do it, too.

CHAPTER FOUR

The Effects of Domestic Violence on Children

Children raised in abusive situations often feel both guilt and anger about the violence in their lives. They can think they are the cause of your partner's abuse. Since the family is the primary environment where we learn to relate to others, parents who fight in front of their children provide violent role models for them. Because they see it in the home, the message to children is that violence, humiliation and disrespect are to be expected in intimate relationships. As Joyce described it:

> One day in the shelter all the kids made drawings for their mothers. I was busy doing something and really not paying much attention to Monte who kept begging me to look at his drawing. Finally I looked at it. It was a picture of two people yelling "shut up" at each other.

Girls in violent homes may come to believe that all men are abusive and that women are naturally abused. Boys may learn that men have a right to batter women. Like their mothers, children raised in violent homes can come to know abuse as caring. They may repeat the pattern of violence by becoming abused or abusive adults. An African-American mother who had expressed great pain and bitterness about the violence in her childhood, still had this to say, "It has been difficult not to be abusive with my own kids because that's the behavior I learned."

According to a shelter worker who conducted interviews with incoming battered women, about forty-five percent of them said their children had been abused, too. The abuse is usually the physical fallout of actions directed toward the woman. However, children in violent homes can also be sexually abused, emotionally threatened and have their young lives put in jeopardy, as Yolanda revealed:

> My husband never actually hit the kids, but he had a gun. He'd leave it lying around and then make comments about how "tragic" it would be if the gun accidentally went off or if one of the kids played with it and killed himself. I was terrified to leave the house. I didn't want to come home and discover my three-year-old had picked the gun up off the coffee table and blown his brains out.

Children often separate their parents during beatings, and the psychological effect can be as damaging as physical injuries they might suffer. Said one abused mother:

> My daughter's speech became impaired and her physical coordination got so bad that she was bumping into and tripping over everything in the apartment. She wasn't my child anymore. She was an old lady living with us trying to keep us from fighting.

Because of the constant upheaval in their lives, your children may have trouble with their schoolwork. They may even develop a fear of school if they've had to be the new kid in class each time leaving your partner has caused them to change schools. You may find that your child may not want to go to sleep at night or reverts to bed-wetting after a violent episode in the home.

Specialized programs with a professional can help children understand that what goes on between you and their father (or your partner) is not their fault. In specialized programs, through the use of dolls and other toys, children are encouraged to express their feelings about the violent behavior they have seen or experienced and to release their feelings about it. They can also learn to control their own rage and to express it constructively.

You may believe that you are "protecting" your children by not talking about it, but the truth is that children need to understand as much as they can about domestic violence — most of all that it is not their fault. Some shelters have children's advocates on staff who conduct play therapy sessions along with coordinating other activities. Find out which ones in your area have advocates and whether children have to live in the shelter to participate in activities.

When you've decided to make some changes to end the violence in your life, consider talking to your child's teacher, school psychologist or social worker about your plans. If they have some understanding of the issues involved in domestic violence they may be able to offer suggestions that can help you and provide support. You might find out if they are familiar with domestic violence by asking them to recommend a book on the topic.

Children are powerless, vulnerable and completely dependent on adults to protect them. Children raised in violent homes see a world that is brutal, painful and often totally out of control. And yet, because it is the only world they know — one which is controlled in their eyes by their parents — they will naturally believe that what they see their parents do is right.

Through play therapy and/or honest explanations from you, your child can be taught to understand but not accept the violence in your home. Your child needs to realize that the violence is wrong and can be stopped. Perhaps while you are in a shelter, living with other abused women and their children, you can exchange ideas about effective ways to talk to children about domestic violence. In fact, it was while in the safety of a shelter support group that La Tonya found the courage to say that her child prompted her to leave an abusive partner.

> When I heard my five-year-old daughter saying, "Stop hitting my mommy," the same thing I'd said twenty years ago when I was a kid, I knew it was time to get help. First it had been my mother, then me, my daughter was next in line. I'm here because I don't want my daughter to be battered. I need to change my life so hers can be better.

Research shows that with some type of counseling, most children are resilient enough to withstand the effects of domestic violence. All is not hopeless if your children have watched you be abused. Children need not repeat the learned pattern of abuse that disrupts their young lives. They can live happy, healthy and productive lives — free from abuse and violence.

CHAPTER FIVE

How to Protect Yourself

There are helping professionals who can assist you in the process of ending the violence in your life. It doesn't cost a thing for you to call the police or go to a battered women's shelter if your partner is threatening to harm you. You can get the best service from the resources available to you if you understand their views and practices regarding abused women. It is possible to receive competent and compassionate service from police, health professionals and shelter workers that you might go to for help.

Police

The most immediate resource for an abused Black woman in an emergency or life-threatening situation is the police.

What to Expect

Police attitudes about domestic violence have generally reflected those of the larger culture, and as the culture changes so do police attitudes. Some police officers believe that men have a right to hit women, that women "provoke" men into violent acts, that a man is "king of the castle," and that a woman who stays with an abusive man must "like" being beaten. Police are not immune to the sexist and racist ideas that pervade our society.

Two of the most common beliefs and the ones most likely to affect your interaction with the police as an abused African-

American woman are 1) domestic violence is a private "family matter" in which the police shouldn't interfere and 2) violence is a "natural" part of Black culture. Frances, a woman with a ten-year history of abuse from her husband, recounted these kinds of experiences with the police:

> They didn't give a damn, they just didn't care. They could see I was pregnant and that he had beaten me. But do you think they talked to me? They took him [batterer] outside for a while. I looked out the window, and they were all just laughing and joking. The police were standing there admiring *his van.*

Asked if over the years African-American officers had been more sensitive and willing to help her than whites, she replied,

> Black officers don't want to arrest another Black man, because they know that it could just as easily be them that's going to jail. It's hard. I understand their position. But hell, understanding is not stopping me from getting beat.

Research indicates that responding to domestic violence calls is one of the leading causes of police injuries and deaths. For this reason some police officers dislike domestic violence complaints. Because they do not necessarily understand the battering cycle, some officers also develop poor attitudes about responding week after week to the same violent household where nothing ever changes and charges are never filed.

The role of the police in domestic violence situations can be a frustrating one for all concerned. However, the more you know about police perspectives (right or wrong), the better prepared you'll be when you call on them for help.

Changes

Thanks to activists within the battered women's and other feminist movements, police departments are making efforts to better address the many kinds of violence against women and children: rape, incest and domestic violence. Police officers nationwide are being trained to understand their racism, sexism and homophobia (fear and prejudice against gays and lesbians) and how to change their attitudes so they can more effectively do their work. Some are beginning to understand and respond sympathetically to abused women like Charlotte.

> I told the officer I wanted to press charges, and so he started escorting my husband out the door. As they were leaving, my husband said to the kids, "See what your mother's doing to me." And the officer said, "Leave the kids out of it, you did it to yourself." And then my husband said, "She should quit saying what she says to me." The officer said, "I don't care what she says, man, you keep your hands to yourself." Then he put him out the door and took him downtown. I was shocked.

Slowly but surely, police officers are beginning to realize that an act that traumatizes children, leaves women mentally and physically bruised, and could ultimately result in the officers' own injury or death, is much more than a "family matter." With increased training and continued community pressure, police officers are gradually learning to ask an abused woman if she has any injuries instead of "Who started the fight?"; to suggest that she press charges instead of "kiss and make up." They are learning to hold batterers accountable for breaking the law.

Dealing with the Police

Though it is obviously difficult in an intense, life-threatening situation, you should try to remain as calm as possible when you call the police. Explain that you are being assaulted and give your address slowly and accurately. It is not important that the police know it is your partner who is beating you. This may cause them to ignore the call or respond more slowly because of their attitudes about domestic violence. Let the police know immediately if there is a weapon involved. They need to know where you are, that you believe you're in danger and need emergency help.

It is impossible to predict how your partner will respond when you call the police. Some men leave quickly, some become more abusive, others wait calmly for the police to arrive so they can state their case. The important things to remember are that 1) you have as much a right to be protected from an abusive partner as you do from a violent stranger on the streets, 2) police officers have a duty to do their jobs regardless of personal attitudes they might have about domestic violence or Black people, 3) the job of the police is to respond to and prevent crime, and 4) domestic violence is a crime.

Arrest

Recent studies on domestic violence have shown that police arrests of batterers can cut repeat battering in half.

The laws in your state will determine whether your partner is arrested for assaulting you. A few states have a mandatory arrest law, meaning the police are legally bound to arrest your abuser within a certain time period if there is evidence he has assaulted you. A mandatory arrest law prevents the police from merely driving your partner around or suggesting that he take a walk after he has assaulted you until he "cools down." It has proven to be an effective tool for altering patterns of abuse.

In other states, the police have the option of making an arrest if they have "probable cause" (visible weapons, injuries, witnesses) to believe your partner has assaulted you. They are also likely to arrest him if he assaults you in their presence, if he attacks them, if he has violated a "no contact" or restraining order (see Chapter 6), or if there are outstanding warrants for his arrest.

If the police do not arrest your partner, that does not mean that there is nothing they can do to help you. When responding to a domestic violence call, police can administer first aid to you, establish and maintain the peace, write a thorough report of the incident, give you information about counseling, housing, legal assistance and medical treatment, and transport you to a battered women's shelter, medical facility or home of a relative or friend.

The police cannot force your partner to leave your house permanently, give you disputed money or property, settle child custody matters or force your partner to go into alcohol, drug or batterer's counseling.

The Police Report

It is very important that the police take an accurate and complete report of the incident between you and your partner. The police report can influence later decisions you might make about prosecution.

Describe the assault in detail, and make sure the officers see your injuries. You may have to explain to them that bruises on African-Americans are not always as visible or look as dramatic as they do on white people. Tell the police if your partner threatened or actually used a weapon during the assault. They also need to know if he has violated probation, if there are outstanding warrants for his arrest and if he has a history of drug or alcohol abuse. Tell the police the names and the addresses of the people who witnessed your partner assault you. Give physical evidence of the assault, such as torn clothing or broken household items, to the police. After the police have finished taking the report, ask them for the case number of the report.

Should you choose to prosecute your partner for assaulting you, the police report will be an important factor in the case. In addition, it serves as an official document of his violent behavior. It shows your partner that you do not take his abuse lightly and that it is a serious crime.

Your partner may protest about police brutality against Blacks or accuse you of "betraying" the race by calling them. There is no denying that the relationship between the police and the African-American community has been problematic. Historically, the police have been some of the worst offenders in contributing to or blatantly ignoring the violence in Black communities. The most important thing to remember is that your safety is more important than any kind of racial loyalty. Police intervention will stop your partner's immediate violent actions against you.

Medical Help

If you have been seriously injured during an assault, the police should give you immediate assistance or call an aid car to take you to a medical facility. Unless you live in a remote, rural area, chances are there will be other African-Americans in the emergency room. Contrary to certain beliefs, this is not because violence is a natural part of Black people's lives. The stress of urban living often contributes to mental and physical problems for Blacks that demand emergency medical treatment.

What To Do

When you arrive at the medical facility, let the admitting person know that you have been hurt in a domestic dispute and ask if there is anyone on staff who deals with battered women. Perhaps there is an African-American woman you can talk to, but don't feel discouraged if there is not. Describe your pain and injuries as completely as you can to the person who is treating you. Ask for photographs to be taken of your injuries. Because bruises on dark skin might not photograph very clearly, make sure that detailed notes are also taken.

If your batterer comes to the emergency room with you, you may be afraid to tell the truth about how you received your injuries. You may be afraid of what he might do to you later or what might happen to him. You can request that a staff person ask him to leave. Though you may be very confused, frightened or worried about him, remember that your safety and immediate treatment of the injuries *he* caused should come first. You have every right to explain what he has done to you without him being around.

After your immediate medical needs have been attended to and before you are released, be sure to ask for and write down the names of the emergency room staff members who have treated you. This should include doctors, nurses, social workers, clerks and any police officers who may have been called to the hospital if someone else brought you there. Later you should prepare a special envelope to keep all medical bills and receipts for medication or supplies you had to purchase as a result of your injuries. For instance, you might need major dental work to replace lost teeth or a new pair of eyeglasses if your partner broke yours during the assault. Be sure to save the receipts for such items.

Even if your injuries do not require emergency medical treatment, they should be checked out as soon as possible after the incident. Though you may not see them or feel them, you could have internal injuries, as one abused woman found out.

> My wrist hurt a little bit after he beat me up, but I didn't think it was anything serious. But the days went by, and it just didn't get better. Finally, it got so bad I could barely grip the brush to comb my daughter's hair. So I went to the doctor, where I found out my wrist was actually broken.

It is important to go to the doctor because what you may think is just a sore, swollen limb may turn out to be broken bone that needs to be set.

Visit your family doctor, and explain that your injuries are a result of domestic violence. If you don't have a doctor, are embarrassed to talk about the abuse, or feel that you can't afford to see a doctor unless you are "really" sick, make an appointment at a local women's health clinic. You can usually find one by calling the YWCA or an agency in your community that assists women who have been raped. There is no guarantee, but the staff at a women's health clinic is likely to be more understanding of your attitudes and experiences as an abused Black woman.

Abused African-American women may encounter both the myths and stereotypes about Black women as well as those about all battered women when we seek medical help. These include: we like being beaten; we provoke our abuser; we are castrating bitches, sexually promiscuous, accustomed to violence and probably welfare mothers who don't care about our health until we are in crisis.

Given these attitudes, it is not surprising that we are sometimes reluctant to be treated by white health care workers or to discuss our battering experiences with them. The American health care system, dominated as it is by white males, has historically been insensitive to our needs.

Remember, however, that you should never be made to feel ashamed, foolish or responsible for your abuse when you seek medical help. You are not to blame for your injuries and what you deserve is compassionate care, not unsympathetic lectures from health care professionals.

If you do not feel confident or comfortable enough to see someone by yourself, ask a trusted and assertive friend to accompany you. The friend can supply moral support and serve as a witness to your injuries and the type of medical treatment you were given. If you are reluctant to have bruised private parts of your body examined, your friend can take photographs of them before or after you are treated professionally.

Your physical health and safety are the most important reasons for you to seek medical treatment after your partner has assaulted you. Additionally, documented evidence of his abuse can help your case should you decide to prosecute. Your accumulation of medical evidence (no matter how small) may stop your partner from striking you if he thinks medical reports might be used later in court.

Shelters

"Nowhere to run to, baby, nowhere to hide" describes the plight of an abused woman searching for shelter prior to the mid-1970s. There was simply no place to go. Fortunately, through the efforts of thousands of women, including many formerly battered ones, a much-needed shelter network has developed over the past twenty years.

There are an estimated 1200 battered women's shelters across the country. Though often forced to survive on minimal financial resources, battered women's shelters have been vital forces in saving and redirecting the course of many women's and children's lives.

Shelters are designed to insure the safety of the women and children who stay in them for a few days, a few weeks, or up to a month. Shelter locations are usually known only to staff and the local police. The most important reason for you to go to a battered women's shelter is that it provides safety and protection from the person who is abusing you. Family members or friends may encourage you to stay with your abusive partner (in the tradition of "strong Black womanhood") or to forgive him and eventually go back. In a shelter, however, you will be supported by other abused women who want you to make the best decision you can that will eliminate the violence from your life. As Camille said:

> There was so much stress and pressure at home — from him and my friends to "work it out." So being at the shelter was like a vacation. The kids and I just didn't have to deal with that. I could finally think about what I wanted to do.

The daily routine in a shelter will vary depending on the policies it has. However, in almost all, the cooking, cleaning, childcare and other household duties will be shared by residents on a rotating schedule. You can expect house meetings, counseling sessions and group activities, all designed to undo some of the damage of your partner's abuse and to help you make independent decisions about your future life.

The shelter will be staffed by women who can help you with questions about housing, jobs, counseling, education, health and childcare. In urban areas, there are often African-American women on shelter staffs, including some who may have been battered at one time themselves. These women will be at the shelter with you twenty-four hours a day to help you as best they can.

Just as important as the guidance you will receive from shelter staff is the confidence and knowledge you'll gain from living with other abused women who understand your situation because they have experienced it too. As Joy said:

> I really didn't want to go but being in the shelter really helped me a lot. Sure there were some personality problems and rules I didn't like. But I didn't get hit for not liking them, and my son was not scared. The counselors allowed him to express his feelings openly. Besides being safe, one of the most helpful things I learned in the shelter was how to deal with my anger when my son misbehaves.

Much of your isolation, your feeling that you are perhaps the only abused Black woman in the world, will begin to change when you meet other African-American women like yourself. In the shelter you will also meet women of other races with different backgrounds and experiences from your own. You will meet women who have perhaps held down jobs, gone to school, found new apartments — all while being abused. You will learn from them that you are indeed capable of changing your life and doing things that your partner has told you you cannot do. Living with and sharing experiences with other abused women will show you that abuse does not happen only to Black women, but to women from all walks of life. Most important, it will show you that support from other abused women can inspire you to change your life.

Although you can learn much from the diversity of the shelter staff and residents, sharing living space with different kinds of people and following shelter rules may cause you some frustration. Because shelters are not immune to the racism that exists in society, some can be run in ways that are insensitive to the cultural needs or perspectives of African-American women. Sandra remembered this about her shelter experience:

> Some of the counselors can treat you like you're crazy or stupid. You can feel imprisoned or like a child. I'm a grown woman. And I'm going through enough as it is without having to go through stuff with counselors.

As an abused Black woman, you may be reluctant to leave a familiar network of neighbors, family and friends to go live in a shelter with a group of people you don't know much about or have been taught to mistrust. If the shelter happens to be located in a white neighborhood you may feel vulnerable, visible and unprotected.

Although the extended family is indeed a part of our culture and tradition, you may not be accustomed to or like the communal style of living in shelters. You may find it uncomfortable to sleep in the same room, share bathrooms and change clothes in front of strangers from different races or ethnicities. Because of our history as domestic workers, you may take offense at the requirement that you cook meals, clean and perform childcare duties for other shelter residents, some of whom may be white. You may not understand why alcohol and non-prescription drugs are not allowed or why you will be forbidden to spank your child, as is the case in most shelters. You may not like the curfews or signing-out systems that many shelters have to make sure residents are always accounted for. You may disagree with the rule that you can't even tell your best girlfriend the address of the shelter.

Although you may feel like they were made up specifically to oppress you, most shelter rules exist for a reason — to keep violent and potentially dangerous men away from the women and children they have abused. "If one woman tells her partner where the shelter is, it can affect the whole group," said a counselor. "Many women fear revenge from any man who comes near the shelter. It's contagious."

However, if the shelter has rules that you feel disregard your feelings or experiences as a Black woman, do not be afraid to discuss it in a house meeting or with an individual staff member. You can use the experience to get back some of the sense of power your partner has driven out of you as well as to help foster the cultural sensitivity that will make shelters and other service agencies more responsive to the needs of African-American women. Talk up if you are made to feel uncomfortable about the kind of food you cook, the music you listen to or the way you comb your children's hair. A simple comment like, "I'd rather do yardwork or answer phones today instead of cooking because too much time in the kitchen makes me feel like a maid," will point out to other shelter residents that you are willing to do your fair share of chores, but not at the expense of your self-esteem.

You may feel uneasy speaking up for yourself because of your experiences with an abusive partner. Remember that though you may experience conflicts, communication problems or blatant racist incidents while in the shelter, no one is going to batter you for expressing your feelings.

Some abused women, like Paula, report that they made friends for life while at a battered women's shelter.

> It just seemed like Diane and I had so much in common. I found out we'd even cussed out the same police officers. In the shelter we'd help each other out with the kids and trying to find apartments and just doing all the stuff that seems so hard unless there's somebody who understands. I eventually went to my mother's, but Diane and I stayed in touch and we do to this day.

There are many different types of shelters. Some are run by church groups, the YWCA or the Salvation Army; others by women's organizations, the local city government or non-profit groups.

To find out about shelter services in your area, check the telephone listings (often located at the front of the book with other emergency numbers) under "Battered" or "Abused Women." Your local police department or community crisis line should also be able to give you information about shelters. You might want to write down all these numbers and put them in a safe place.

After your safety, the greatest benefit of staying in a shelter is that you will meet other abused women like yourself. With their support, you can laugh, cry and begin to work toward ending the violence in your life.

CHAPTER SIX

The Legal System

A general understanding of how women have been viewed within the legal system will help you feel less threatened and more in control when dealing with legal professionals about the violence in your life. With an understanding of some of its practices and traditions, you can make the system serve you better as an abused African-American woman.

Blacks and the Legal System

English common law, which America inherited when the country was founded, contributes to the tolerance of violence against women within our legal system today. Seventeenth-century English common law held "by rule of thumb" that a man could beat a woman with a rod no thicker than his thumb. The routine beating of women went unchallenged because women were not considered human beings, but rather property. This tradition of male "ownership" and domination of others still exists in our culture today. For example, boats and cars are commonly referred to by the pronoun "she." The most devastating example, however, of people legally transformed into property was the Black American experience of slavery.

Through a combination of racist attitudes and the legal system, white males were able to rationalize and maintain their control over Black people during slavery. Blacks, because of our dark skin, were viewed as savage, dangerous and naturally inferior to whites. Whites believed that slavery tempered the "heathen" tendencies of Blacks and tamed what they believed to be our unrestrained sexuality. Because whites refused to believe that Blacks were capable of loving or forming emotional bonds with each other, marriage between slaves was not legally binding.

These beliefs helped whites rationalize their cruel and systematic destruction of African-American families. By their thinking, since we couldn't love like other human beings, what did it matter if a child was torn from his or her mother and sold away? In the poem, "Slave Auction," from her 1854 collection *Poems on Miscellaneous Subjects,* early Black abolitionist Frances E.W. Harper addresses the plight of slave women:

And mothers stood with streaming eyes,
And saw their dearest children sold,
Unheeded rose their bitter cries,
While tyrants bartered them for gold...

Essentially, a slave was considered to have no more legal authority over a child than a cow over her calf. Black women were thus reduced to the level of domestic animals. Just as a brood mare could not be raped or abused, neither could a Black woman.

Fortunately the official laws that permitted wife-beating and slavery no longer exist. But it would be naive to think that those sexist and racist attitudes don't still influence the American justice system. Blacks have learned through countless painful experiences that not all people are created equal and not everyone receives equal protection under the law.

Reasons To Use the Legal System

Though you may be reluctant to "bring down the law" on another Black person, the legal system can protect you and help you feel less victimized by the man who is abusing you. If you were injured by a stranger, you would probably phone the police, report it and find out your legal options. Taking such action would make you feel more powerful and could possible deter the stranger from assaulting someone else. You can look at the situation between you and an abusive partner in the same light. The laws that give you legal protection against a violent stranger also apply to the man who is abusing you. There is no question that African-American men have suffered discrimination at the hands of racist judges and attorneys. But the laws that protect you from domestic violence are not laws against Black men. They are laws against crime.

There is always the possibility that a judge or attorney might make a racist comment or tell you to be a "better wife" should you use the legal system to stop the abuse in your life. On the other hand, there is the certainty that you will be abused again if you do not take some step toward letting your partner know that his behavior is unacceptable and indeed against the law. One option you might consider is filing for a restraining order.

Restraining Orders

A restraining order is an official court document designed to prevent violence by one member of a household against another. All states in the country have passed laws that make the order available to you. Although the filing procedures and fees may vary depending on where you live, you will usually not have to hire a lawyer to get a restraining order. The charges for it are often minimal or can be waived if you have a low income. In some states the court can order your partner to repay you for the costs of obtaining a restraining order.

A restraining order prohibits your partner from threatening, striking or harassing you. Depending on state law, it can also protect you and give you temporary custody of your children, order your partner out of your home and/or to enter a counseling program. If any part of the order is violated, your partner can be jailed, fined or both. The police have the responsibility to enforce your restraining order.

How to Get the Document

The process for obtaining a restraining order usually involves filing forms and later testifying about your abuse before a judge in a court hearing. Your partner will be notified that you have filed for the order and will also be asked to attend the hearing. Hearing testimony from both of you will enable the judge to issue an order that is based on as much information as possible about your relationship.

Your state laws will determine how long your restraining order is effective and the procedures you must follow if you decide to change or terminate it. You can find out specific guidelines about restraining orders in your state by contacting a legal aid clinic, a battered women's shelter or the local police.

Other Legal Options

If you decide to take legal action, there are two separate and distinct legal systems that can provide assistance for you: criminal and civil. Criminal law involves crimes against the state such as assault, murder, rape, theft, property destruction and prostitution. Civil law involves disputes between private parties. This includes processes such as civil restraining orders, divorce, child custody, support payments, property rights, malpractice, personal injury, etc.

If you decide to press charges against your abuser, you will enter the criminal justice system. If there is sufficient evidence that a crime has been committed, then a prosecutor for the state will begin proceedings free of charge, on your behalf. This is why it is very important that accurate and detailed police reports be taken. The description of injuries in the report, photographs, medical records, witness accounts, the presence of weapons and any previous history of violence in your relationship will be critical factors in determining whether your partner is convicted of a crime and the type of sentence he receives.

Benefits of Prosecution

The purpose of prosecution is not to put batterers in jail or deny Black men their "manhood," but rather to begin a process that helps stop violence in your home. In most states once charges are filed a "no contact" or restraining order can be issued, preventing your partner from contacting you before the trial. This can give you time to think about your situation and make plans to improve your life without his menacing presence. If he is found guilty of abusing you, the order can be extended for a specified amount of time. Instead of jail time, the court can order that he complete batterer's and/or alcohol/drug counseling, pay for your medical treatment or damaged property, perform community service hours, pay court costs or serve probation. And of course the court can rule that he spend some time in jail depending on the severity of your injuries and what kind of record your partner has.

The major benefit of prosecution is that it forces your partner to take responsibility for his abusive actions and begin working toward change. He may say you "made" him hit you, that you are putting him in jail, that you don't understand him and that the entire world is against him because he's a Black male. The truth is that he is responsible for choosing violence when he is under stress and he must learn that violence is not acceptable behavior.

Prosecution serves several other important functions aside from forcing your partner to take responsibility for abusing you. Prosecution is a positive action that can raise your self-esteem and help you take control of your life. You begin to move out of the helpless "victim" role when you take the abusive situation out of his hands and into your own. The court process can help you begin to examine feelings about being abused that you may have repressed. Internalized feelings of anger, shame, guilt and self-hatred may begin to surface, enabling you to release them and heal. You may feel truly empowered because you have taken a step toward change. Regardless of the outcome, the trial can serve as a symbolic ending to your abuse. You will have shown your partner that you will no longer be passive and take his abuse. The prospect of standing in front of another judge may make him think twice before striking you again.

Civil Cases

The prosecutor will not be able to help you with divorce, support payments, or settling child custody/visitation rights because they are not criminal matters. For these legal problems you will need to hire a private civil attorney.

Choosing a Civil Attorney

Attorneys' fees are expensive, ranging from $75 to several hundred dollars per hour, so it's important to hire one who will be supportive of you as an abused Black woman. It is easy to feel intimidated by an attorney's language or attitude. But remember you are paying the fee and therefore deserve to be treated professionally. If the attorney you hire ignores your request for explanations or to be regularly informed of the status of your case, then hire a new one. You don't have to give your money to someone who treats you like you don't have any sense.

It might be helpful to prepare a list of questions to determine if the attorney will be supportive of you. These are a few you might want to ask:

1. What services will I be charged for and when do you expect payment?
2. Have you ever helped an abused woman before?
3. Will you answer my questions even though they may seem irrelevant or unimportant to you?
4. Will you understand if I have to bring my children with me to your office on occasion?
5. Will you inform me if there are critical decisions that need to be made about my case?

The responses to these questions should give you a clear idea if your attorney is willing to give you competent and compassionate service.

Legal Aid, lawyer referral agencies, women's groups and Black organizations like the Urban League are usually the best sources for information about low-cost private attorneys. If there is a major university in your city, it probably has a law school. Call the law school and ask if students run a legal clinic in the community. You can also find self-help legal materials in libraries and bookstores that explain how to do some legal procedures yourself.

Even an attorney who charges minimal fees will probably be asking for more money than your budget allows. It may seem unfair that you can't get help because you can't afford it. And because so many abused women need an attorney when they are in crisis, your sense of urgency and desperation may make the situation seem even more unfair. This is because many of us have been raised with the belief that lawyers uphold social morals, battle injustices and always help the "down and out." This is to some extent true. However, the legal profession is also a business — one in which women, minorities, the poor and the disadvantaged are frequently left out. The best way to deal with this situation is to know from the beginning what you are up against financially. You may have to start saving up for your divorce as you would for college tuition or to purchase a new household item. Ask other women if they have hired attorneys who they felt were particularly helpful. Find out if you can set up payment plans with your attorney. A friend or family member who might not loan you money for other things might be happy to pay for legal assistance that will help you end the violence in your life.

It is not unusual to become very close to someone who is helping you with emotional issues like child custody and divorce. Your attorney will no doubt come to know many intimate details about your life. It is important to remember, however, that you have hired the attorney to provide you with supportive legal services, not to be your counselor or personal friend.

Avoid the temptation to make unnecessary personal phone calls (almost all attorneys charge for telephone consultation) or to seek non-legal advice from your attorney. If you contact your attorney too often for non-legal matters, you may get your feelings hurt as well as a bill for what you thought was just "friendly conversation." Remember the attorney has many other clients and is often in court most of the day. She or he may not be able to return your calls or see you should you drop by the office without an appointment. Your attorney has been trained and hired to give you legal assistance and, though concerned about you, may feel uncomfortable when asked to provide other kinds of advice. If you are feeling depressed, anxious, sad, or angry (all natural feelings) about an upcoming trial or life in general, a battered women's advocate or professional counselor can provide support for you.

Advocates

An advocate is a person who serves as an intermediary between abused women and the police, prosecutors, counselors, doctors, etc. The advocate is specially trained in the social and legal issues of domestic violence and will work with you to help make positive changes in your life. She or he will interview you and witnesses (though not usually your partner) about an abusive incident, gather medical records and photographs, explain procedures to you and may process paperwork such as "no contact" or restraining orders.

You can ask the advocate to take you to a courtroom to familiarize you with the surroundings before your case comes up for trial. The advocate can help overworked prosecutors investigate and understand the specific details of your case and thus improve the chances that there will be a positive outcome for you at the trial. She or he may be able to make recommendations to the court about what methods of treatment (i.e., jail, batterer's counseling, fines) would make your partner take responsibility for his actions and stop abusing you.

An advocate can boost your morale and provide reassurance during the tense times before a trial (often four to six weeks), when there may be great pressure on you to return to your partner or to drop the charges that have been filed against him. Some prosecutors have "no-drop" policies to help take some of this pressure off abused women. Others believe that abused women should be allowed to drop the charges if they so decide, simply because they have been forbidden most of their lives to make independent choices or because they are truly terrified by what their partners have threatened to do if the case goes to trial. In any event, the advocate will be there to answer your questions and listen to your fears. As Jeanine said:

> I had times when I wanted to drop the charges. I'd talk to him, and he'd say he was going to go to jail for sure this time. And what good would he be in jail if he couldn't work, is what I thought. He'd say he was trying to get in a drug program, trying to straighten up, and it sounded convincing to me. Everytime I called and tried to drop the charges, the advocate wouldn't let me. So I went ahead with the trial because I didn't have a choice. And I'm glad I did it.

You can call your city prosecutor's office to find out if battered women's advocates are on staff. Advocates also work with shelters, police departments, hospitals and victims assistance programs. In addition to the prosecutor's office you might phone a battered women's shelter, rape crisis line, feminist organization, legal service agency or the social work department of a hospital to ask if there is an advocate to assist you.

What to Expect in the Courtroom

The laws of the city or state you live in and the specific circumstances of your case will determine how the trial proceeds. Your partner will have the option of choosing a bench trial (a judge hears the evidence and decides the verdict) or a jury trial in which you may or may not have to testify. Sometimes prosecutors will attempt to work out a plea bargain with your partner's attorney because of the volume of domestic violence cases. In such an arrangement, your partner may plead guilty to simple assault instead of assault, for example, and not go ahead with a trial. You should be consulted by the prosecutor before such a decision is made. Your safety or personal wishes should not be disregarded just because there's a need to keep things moving in court.

If you do have to testify during the trial, you may want friends or family members to be present in the courtroom. Your abuser may have asked some of his acquaintances to come, and their presence might be frightening or intimidating to you. Try to identify people in your life who will be supportive during what could be an unnerving process, and ask them to come.

Your manner of dress, choice of words and attitude can reinforce or change stereotypes court officials or jurors might have about abused women. You can prepare for that by asking advice from friends who've been to court or an advocate. The most important thing to remember is to be honest in court. No matter what happens during the proceeding, you will feel good about yourself and appear to be a believable witness if you listen carefully, speak clearly, remain calm and simply tell the truth about what happened to you.

There are many reasons why you might feel reluctant to use the legal system to stop your partner from abusing you. You might fear retaliation or that he might go to jail or lose his job. Perhaps you don't want your children to testify in court or you feel that you will be ridiculed and intimidated on the witness stand. You may simply not trust judges, juries and attorneys who have historically discriminated against African-American people. All of these feelings are legitimate, so do not be ashamed or afraid to express them. Simply remember that if you choose to use the legal system it does not mean you are a "traitor" to the race or that there will be no one to support you in your decision. You have every right to take control of your life, and there are many people who are willing to help you.

CHAPTER SEVEN

Helping Hands

After having your emergency needs attended to or taking legal action, you might find that you are still confused or frightened about the abuse in your life. Although the violence has stopped, you may be wondering if you'll ever feel like a "normal" human being or if you'll be able to become involved in another relationship. You can get in touch with your feelings and learn skills that will help you through the next stages of your life by seeing a professional counselor. Support groups, relatives, friends and your church can also be of help to you when you're feeling overwhelmed by your experiences as an abused woman.

Counseling

Because you can still get up and go to work every morning or get the kids off to school, you may feel that you are coping well with the abuse in your life. And you should feel proud of yourself for being able to function in a violent and unpredictable household. But you should also know that you do not have to carry the burden alone. There is nothing wrong with asking for help when you feel you can no longer cope. There are trained counselors who can help you deal with the effects of the physical and emotional abuse in your life.

All humans experience mild forms of depression at some point during their lives. The depression can usually be traced to a specific event and leaves after a short while. If, however, you are unable to sleep or find yourself feeling sad, hopeless, dejected, anxious or crying uncontrollably for extended periods of time, you may need professional help. This does not mean that you are crazy or that you are having a nervous breakdown. It simply means that you have been affected by the violence in your life and with good reason. You *would* be crazy if you thought you could be punched and degraded regularly, but come out unscathed.

Living with violence creates emotional problems that not even you and your mother or best girlfriend can sort out. Counseling is nothing to be ashamed of or to fear. You owe it to yourself to get help.

Finding a Counselor

> From day to day, I, Black Woman, continue to bear the brunt of racism and sexism wherever I go. Oh, to be able to *choose* not to be confronted with one or the other, or both, on any given day — now, that would be the Life.
>
> Who, then, can I turn to when I hurt, real bad? I recall a spiritual that says, "no hidin' place down here." I find myself at therapy's doorstep. Will this counselor usher me to insanity? Because if she does not openly deal with the fact that there is a very low premium on every aspect of my existence, if she does not acknowledge the politics of Black-womanhood, now that would surely drive me nuts.[1]
>
> — Eleanor Johnson

Finding a Black counselor or one who has worked with Black clients may be difficult. It is only recently that Blacks, in sizable numbers, have begun to use our own therapeutic models based on the African-American experience instead of those of the white establishment. As a result, many Blacks no longer shun mental health service systems, but look to them as a means of maintaining good physical and emotional health.

Probably the best place to start your search for a caring, competent counselor is with other Black women friends and co-workers. Ask if they know a local counselor you could see. There are probably community mental health agencies in your area that you can contact. Also check with the National Black Women's Health Project, the YWCA, a battered women's shelter or another women's organization to find out if there is a women's therapy referral service in your community. The therapists who list with a referral service usually offer reduced or sliding-scale fees that allow you to pay for counseling according to your income. Many also grant a free initial interview for you to discuss your issues with the therapist and determine if she or he is suited to your needs. Check the telephone listings under "mental health," "psychology," "feminist," "women," "battering," and "rape" for information about counseling. You can also call your community crisis line and explain you are looking for a counselor who helps abused women. They may have someone on file who can assist you. Ask your family doctor if she or he can refer you to someone. There will undoubtedly be one counselor somewhere with whom you'll feel comfortable discussing your problems and feelings.

If you are thinking about seeing a male counselor, consider that you have been conditioned to view them as experts and authority figures. Those same views of men as all powerful and all knowing have contributed to society's acceptance of domestic violence.

A Black male counselor, although more acceptable racially, may not be sensitive to your position as an abused Black woman. He may identify with the attitudes and experiences of the man who is abusing you. He may not be able to listen to you objectively, though as a professional, he should surely try. Because he understands our racial pressures and oppressions, a Black male counselor can be as invested in keeping the African-American family together as you are. He may encourage you to "bear up," "be strong," "keep the faith" or work it out with your partner for the sake of the children and the race. But your counselor does not have to go home and live with an abusive partner like you do. He does not have to worry about how he's going to "keep the faith" while trying to keep the peace too.

A Black woman counselor who understands and is sensitive to the issues involved in domestic violence would be ideal. However, if she is not to be found, chances are you will have to consider seeing a white woman counselor.

Regardless of gender or race, the counselor you ultimately choose should treat you professionally. Although some of your experiences might be similar to those of other abused women, your counselor should attempt to get to know you as an individual, rather than offer treatment based on stereotypical views about abused women.

There are certain practices that are generally considered completely unethical. For instance, if your counselor approaches you sexually or does not maintain the confidentiality of your therapeutic relationship, you have every right to leave that counselor and even report the behavior. However, other practices that might also be harmful to you may not be so obvious. A few guidelines can help insure that your counselor does not do additional damage to you because of a lack of understanding of domestic violence or your perspectives as an African-American woman.

Under no circumstances should you continue to see a counselor who tells you violence is a natural part of Black life; who says you provoked your partner; who does not believe you are in serious danger when you say you are; who makes fun of the way you express yourself; who uses any kind of racial slur; who forces you to try counseling techniques that make you uncomfortable; or who suggests you relieve the stress in your life with alcohol, drugs or increased sexual activity.

If you have never had counseling before, locating a therapist and beginning the process of sharing and self-disclosure may "work your last nerve." You may be terrified to talk with a stranger about your problems. You may wonder if you are being judged or if what you say is "right." The key to all your concerns is trust, and building a trusting relationship with a counselor does not happen overnight.

Developing trust with your counselor depends on several things: your counselor's skills and techniques, the manner in which you present your problems, your personal commitment to the counseling process, and what you expect to get out of counseling. It may be a good idea to evaluate these issues before you start seeing someone regularly.

Talking It Out

There will be times when you perhaps feel worse after a session than you did before you talked to your counselor. As one abused woman said, you may leave asking yourself, "I pay money for *this?*" Ironic as it may seem, it is probably when you ask yourself that question that the healing process has begun.

At first, you may talk to your counselor only about "safe" things like your job, family, hobbies or activities you did during the week. However, as the process continues and you begin to trust your counselor, you are likely to reveal experiences that really hurt or puzzled you. You may find yourself telling your counselor something you hadn't thought about in years or something you thought was completely unimportant to you. This is because in order to survive in an abusive relationship you have had to steel yourself against really feeling your emotions. You have probably repressed mountains of rage, resentment, shame, helplessness, disgust and guilt about being abused. As you develop a trusting relationship with your counselor these powerful feelings will start to surface. And when you express your feelings, you'll begin to heal.

Therapy can be a very difficult and emotionally draining process. It can also help you regain your strength and sense of power. Unlike the abuse you have suffered, counseling will not kill you. The key to a successful experience is commitment, caring and trust between you and your therapist.

Support Groups

In addition to, or sometimes instead of, individual counseling, you should consider participating in a support group for abused women. A support group provides exactly what the name says — support and encouragement for you from other women who know how you feel and understand what you're talking about. They know your issues because they have been in the same situation you have. They've heard the same promises you have and watched them be broken. They've filed charges like you have and dropped them. They've felt low-down, broke-down and put-down like you have. They've thought about killing him like you have, prayed like you have, wondered if they were losing their minds or if the situation would ever get any better — just like you have. As Juanita found out, joining a support group can end your isolation by putting you in touch with those people you thought didn't exist — other abused Black women who have suffered just like you.

> A friend told me about this support group for battered Black women, and I just didn't want to hear about it. My ears were open, but my mind was shut. I was afraid of what people would think — that they would know I was one of 'them.' But I eventually went — I suppose I was so miserable I knew I had to. And it was hard at first just like I thought it would be. But it was *so* good to see other Black faces — to finally talk to other women who'd been in the same situation as me. We laughed, we cried. We talked about everything. It got to the point that those meetings were the highlight of my week. Some of my friends even wanted to go because they saw what a change it made in me. You know, Black women can do a lot of things we think we can't do. Like learning we can be somebody without a man. That we don't have to be beaten up, that our kids don't have to be scared to death. That our pride and our families don't have to be ruined.

Support groups for abused women are part of a growing self-help movement in the country. The rationale behind them is that you know more about your life than anyone else and that the best place for you to look for emotional support and practical help is often from other abused women.

Support groups for abused women vary in their size and organizational structure. Some are led by trained counselors who consider domestic violence their field of expertise. Others are run by grassroots activists who have served leadership roles in the women's movement for many years. And there are of course support groups that are organized and led by formerly abused women. The role of the leader or leaders in all cases is to facilitate the exchange of ideas and experiences between abused women.

Battered women's shelters, churches, community centers or the local YWCA are places where support group meetings are often held. They are usually free, and sometimes childcare is provided.

Many support groups have a "drop-in" format, meaning that meetings are not mandatory. You can choose to attend whenever you want. Sometimes counselors organize abused women's groups for a specific period of time. In these groups, participants may be asked to pay a fee and are usually expected to attend meetings regularly. Efforts are made in all abused women's groups to insure the safety of participants and to maintain confidentiality.

A support group can be a critical factor in helping you develop or reclaim your self-esteem. The strength and humor you see in other African-American women as they talk about the lies they've been told and the slaps they've survived will help you see that you also have those qualities. Likewise, seeing other Black women cry and express their vulnerabilities can free you to let down your defenses and stop being the "strong Black woman."

A support group can help foster feelings of intimacy and trust between African-American women. For too long we have been told and perhaps too many of us have believed that we will talk about each other, steal each other's men and stab each other in the back whenever we get the chance. These myths have lived long and destructive lives. It is time for Black women to put them to rest, or at least begin to talk about them openly.

Being in a support group can give you the courage to stop denying that you are involved with an abusive man and that your life may be in real danger. You can begin to look at your situation objectively and develop approaches to problem-solving that have worked for other African-American women. For instance, you may never think of using your gardening skills for relaxation, exercise or perhaps to supplement your income until you hear it or something similar mentioned in your support group. Because you have heard for so long that you can't do anything, you may indeed forget all the skills and abilities you have. A support group can be a stimulus for growth, change and a reawakening of yourself. If you see other abused Black women making changes in their lives, you'll realize you can do it too — be it following through on prosecution, taking a class, auditioning for a play or going to a movie by yourself. A support group can help you gain a proper perspective on your life. You may have been scared to death, sick to death or almost beaten to death, but in a support group you'll be acknowledged for being a survivor. You'll find much love and support from women who want you to stay alive.

Some facilitators of support groups for abused Black women say that it is sometimes difficult to keep the groups active. You may be reluctant to attend meetings because you fear another woman in the group might know your partner or that your confidentiality will not be honored. You may not want to appear "weak" in front of other African-American women.

There is nothing wrong with having these feelings. But you might also consider a support group as a way you can overcome them and learn how to communicate more effectively with other Black women. By talking about your fears, you can help shatter some of the cultural myths that have kept Black women distant from and suspicious of each other. You can open yourself up to the beauty, wisdom and supportive love of other Black women.

Racially Mixed Groups

Your chances of finding a support group specifically for abused African-American women are best if you live in a large, metropolitan area. However, because not all the resources (human or financial) have been developed to insure the long-term existence of support groups for battered Black women, you may have to attend a racially mixed support group that might be run by a white woman.

Like the abused Black woman who sees a white woman counselor for individual therapy, you may bring some suspicions to a racially mixed support group. Because of relationships between white women and Black men, you may view white group members symbolically as competitors or threats to your relationships. You may be afraid that the information you share in the support group will be used to perpetuate racist views about African-American men. You may be reluctant to talk about racism in front of white women or feel the need to always appear strong. In short, you may simply not believe that it is safe for you to discuss your relationship with a Black man in a racially mixed group.

Perhaps "head-on" is the best way for you to approach this sensitive issue. Share your fears and suspicions with the group leader or individual group members. Ask them to respond to your views. See if they understand your feelings. Ask them and yourself if it is possible to work through the racial barriers that exist.

Trust your intuition as to whether a racially mixed support group will be helpful or harmful to you. Ask other Black women who have participated in such groups to share their experience with you.

Although there may be some added stresses to participating in a racially mixed support group, it can also be a rewarding experience for you. The group can provide an opportunity for you to take a leadership role in initiating discussions about racism and other barriers that exist between women, such as class, religion and sexual preference. There is an additional benefit to participating in a racially mixed support group. It will give you living proof that battering crosses all racial and ethnic boundaries. This commonality of experience can and does help abused women understand that oppressive social systems support violence against all women in our society. It can give you the courage to change your life.

You can get information about support groups from the same sources you contacted about individual counseling — shelters, women's therapy referral services, community mental health agencies and the YWCA.

If you can't find a support group in your community, consider starting one yourself. *Talking It Out* (see Resources) is a book with excellent practical and philosophical information about support groups. If "support group" sounds too serious, you can call your group a circle or some other name. In fact, "Circles of Sisterhood" by Linda Villarosa is an article in the October 1994 issue of *Essence* magazine that highlights the different kinds of support groups Black women have formed around the country. It is possible for you and other women to share your experiences even if there is no organized support group in your community.

Friends and Family

Because of our extended family system, friends and family often overlap in many Black people's lives. Many of us have "play" mothers, fathers, sisters, brothers and cousins who are no blood relation to us, but who may have played a significant role in our upbringing. They are considered as much a part of our family as real aunts, uncles and grandmothers. This support network enriches the African-American community and nurtures us individually as we face the challenges of daily living. It can, however, serve as a double-edged sword, helping and hurting when we go to family or friends about the violence in our lives.

Couples tend to socialize and build relationships with other couples. Chances are that friends you'd choose to speak with about your partner's abusive behavior are friends of his too. They might have divided loyalties and feel you are pressuring them to take sides about your relationship. Your friends may listen, but really not want to interfere in what they consider to be a personal and private matter between you and your partner. Because they want to believe that you are still the happy couple you may outwardly appear to be, your friends may not take your revelations of abuse seriously. This situation can cause you to think you are crazy or stupid for making a big deal out of something your friends listen to calmly. Or else, it may upset you because it might seem that not even your best and most trusted friends care that you are being abused.

The truth is that neither your family nor friends have been trained to identify or understand all the complex issues involved in domestic violence. They may think it is his job or lack of one, his drinking or his jealousy that is causing your partner to assault you. Because abusive men are sometimes outstanding members of the community, your family and friends may only know your partner as a good father, a committed Little League coach — as a man who always brings the paycheck home. Similarly, they may find it hard to believe that a strong and independent woman like you would put up with abuse and therefore suspect you must be doing something to "deserve it" or that you "like it." Their lack of information and misconceptions about domestic violence can make family and friends ineffective resources to help you stop the violence in your life.

On the opposite end of the spectrum of friends and family members who may not seem to care about your abuse are the people who will jump right in and intervene completely for you. These relatives and friends may insist that you call the police, leave your partner immediately or offer to confront him on your behalf. Occasionally such a response can complicate your situation. For example, your partner may refuse to let people who criticize his behavior come to your house.

Despite their good intentions, a friend or relative who tells you what to do or tries to solve all your problems for you is not being very helpful to you. For like the man who is abusing you, they are denying you the opportunity to take charge of your own life. By not allowing you to decide when and how you wish to deal with the violence in your life, they may undermine your sense of confidence and ability to make independent decisions.

Your family and friends probably care a lot about what is happening to you even though their silences, misconceptions or "take charge" tendencies may not provide exactly the kind of help you need. Unless you and your partner have been exceptionally skillful in hiding the difficulties between you, family and friends probably have some idea that there are problems in your household. In fact, many of the people who phone domestic hotlines for information identify themselves as friends or relatives of women who are being abused.

Within their limitations, your friends and family may be positive and supportive resources. Determine who you can go to for emotional comfort, shelter, a warm meal, peace, financial or childcare assistance if need be. But do not expect any of them to end or completely understand the abuse you suffer.

Support from the Church

Instead of seeking active change in the "here and now," some people accept their earthly sufferings and look forward to claiming their reward in heaven. This life, they believe, is a burdensome but necessary cross to bear in order to attain life everlasting. Such is the philosophy of many African-Americans, who because of our oppression and the failings of humanity, have simply chosen to put our trust in the Lord. The spirituals and gospel songs that are an integral part of the Black church, emphasize this theme:

What a friend we have in Jesus
All of our sins and griefs to bear
What a privilege it is to carry
Everything to God in Prayer.

Throughout our history, the church has held a predominant place in Black people's lives. It was a deep, abiding faith in a "greater good" and a "Higher Power" that gave slave families their spiritual strength and unity. They endured the wrenching pain of losing loved ones on the auction block because they had a firm belief that their families would be reunited in another life.

Although we were freed from slavery, "freedom" did not bring

Blacks total access into American life. Denied participation in political activities and enjoying only limited educational, cultural and economic opportunities, we again turned to the church for support that a racist America did not provide. When restaurant owners, motel managers, school officials and real estate agents bolted their doors against us, the church door was wide open. After being brow-beaten and humiliated by white society we could restore our faith and reclaim a sense of dignity through the teachings and activities of the Black church. It is in the church that many of us have developed not only our religious beliefs, but other personal and leadership skills.

Yet religious beliefs or fear of rejection from the church may be keeping you in an oppressive, abusive relationship. As Kim said:

> When he started beating me I went to the elders of the church. They said I couldn't leave him because it would be a bad reflection on them. I didn't want to bring shame on the church. The church and my faith are very important to me.

If you go to your pastor for help about the violence in your life, you may be told to essentially "love, honor and obey" the man who is abusing you. Your pastor may read scriptures to you that perpetuate male dominance over women. This is not necessarily surprising since the church (Black or white) is a male-dominated institution. It is time, however, to begin to challenge those members of the Black clergy who are contributing to the continued abuse of Black women through their lack of knowledge about domestic violence and/or sexist attitudes.

As with the issues of rape and incest, clergy members are only beginning to receive adequate training on domestic violence. It is only in the past decade or so that many of these issues have lost their social stigma. Because Black women usually make up seventy percent of any African-American congregation, it is perhaps more regrettable, but no more surprising, that the Black clergy has been as uninformed about the extent and severity of domestic violence as anyone else.

Perhaps it has been advantageous for your pastor to minimize the domestic violence within the congregation. Just as you may have denied your partner's abusive behavior to save face, your pastor may use silence and denial to continue the social myth that violence simply does not happen in "good Christian families." To acknowledge domestic violence is to admit, some pastors may think, that the church has failed in its mission. It may reflect poorly on your pastor's word and leadership, because domestic violence clearly indicates that there are some wayward sheep in the flock. Black clergy members, often because of their powerful positions within our communities, may be reluctant to make such admissions.

And so, you may be told to accept and forgive the sins of your abusive partner as Christ did for us when he died on the cross. Your pastor may tell you to read Ephesians 5:21, "Wives, submit yourselves unto your own husbands," and urge you to make the sacrifice for your family. You may be told that your abuse is punishment for being spiritually deficient and that if you pray more it will go away. As one abused Black woman reported, your pastor might even say, "Jesus dropped the charges, so why can't you?"

If your pastor encouraged you to read further in Ephesians you'd find:

> Husbands love your wives, just as Christ loved the church and gave himself up for her to make her holy...and to present her to himself as a radiant church, without stain or wrinkle or any other blemish, but holy and blameless. In this same way, husbands ought to love their wives as their own bodies. He who loves his wife loves himself. After all, no one ever hated his own body, but he feeds and cares for it, just as Christ does for the church. (Ephesians 5:25–29)

It is not and never has been God's will that you bow down blindly and accept your partner's abusive behavior. Men who resort to brute force and domination in their relationships deserve strong disapproval and a resounding message that their behavior is wrong from all members of society, including the clergy.

Some church leaders are beginning to confront the real issues of domestic violence and its destructive impact on African-American families. Some are closely affiliated with shelters for battered women or provide meeting rooms for support groups.

The rise of Black women in the clergy has also led to increased information and education about domestic violence. Today women comprise thirty percent of Black divinity school students pursuing degrees leading toward ordination, up from ten percent a decade ago, according to officials at the Interdenominational Theological Center in Atlanta.

Often involved in more socially conscious ministries, Black female clergy members are speaking out about domestic violence and developing programs for abused women. As Rev. Irene Monroe, pastor at the Old Cambridge Bapist Church in Massachusetts says:

> The church has not fulfilled its mission in terms of helping Black women get out of abusive relationships. Instead of empowering sisters, too many Black ministers have supported male domination and kept the yoke around Black women's necks.

Clearly, the total strength of the traditional Black church as a resource for addressing all aspects of violence in our communities has yet to be tapped. Until such time, it is perhaps best for you to remember that scriptures can be interpreted in many ways and that a family in which there is constant upheaval, violence and abuse is not the "holy family" your pastor may urge you to "save."

Perhaps with the support of other Black women in your congregation, you can approach your pastor or other church leaders to invite a speaker or sponsor an educational workshop on domestic violence. Try calling a battered women's shelter for suggestions of people in your community who have spoken to church groups about this issue before. Ask friends you might have from other congregations if they've had such programs at their church. Contact the Center for the Prevention of Sexual and Domestic

Violence (see Resources). It is an interreligious, educational ministry serving both the religious and secular communities.

The words of black poet Ntozake Shange can provide inspiration when you face situations, like an abusive relationship, that challenge your religion or faith:

> *i found god in myself*
> *& i loved her / i loved her fiercely*

CHAPTER EIGHT

Lesbians and Abuse

Most incidents of domestic violence are perpetrated by men against women and children. As noted in previous chapters, society gives men permission to exert power and control within their families.

Women have been conditioned to be passive and nurturing and are generally less prone to acts of violence than are men. However, women involved in same-sex relationships are not immune to battering. For example, Fran Staton, an African-American therapist who practices in Berkeley, California, reports that more than half of her Black lesbian clients have been physically and/or emotionally abused by their female lovers at some point in their lives.

Not only does a lesbian relationship not provide a guarantee against domestic violence, but the secrecy and silence often imposed on the relationship by anti-gay bias in society often make intervention more difficult. Unlike heterosexuals, many gays are unable to live and love openly. Although some states have passed laws prohibiting discrimination against homosexuals, gays and lesbians can still lose jobs, housing and child-custody battles because of their sexual identity. They can still be kicked out of the church and the military because of who they love.

And despite recent gains made by the gay rights movement, many homosexuals still fear rejection from friends and family members if they "come out of the closet" about their sexuality.

For "closeted" lesbians to speak about abuse is to expose a

previously hidden relationship and risk both personal and public censure.

Society also has difficulty accepting the existence of lesbian violence because it disrupts our traditional views about women. We are taught to believe that women are more gentle and understanding than men. We expect them to have good communication skills and an innate ability to "kiss and make it better." That a woman could beat, slap, kick or verbally abuse another woman is unimaginable to us.

Even lesbians themselves have been slow to acknowledge or confront the violence in their community. Denial, a reluctance to fuel anti-gay sentiments and a desire to preserve their own physical and emotional safety are among the reasons that many lesbians have been silent about same-sex abuse.

A coordinator of services for battered lesbians in the San Francisco Bay area says: "Society already thinks our relationships aren't valid, so it's even harder to admit that domestic violence occurs in our relationships, too. I can understand why people don't want to air this dirty laundry. But we can't let fear of negative stereotyping control us."

Additional Burdens

The low self-esteem, lack of confidence and deep need to control that triggers some men to violate their partners also exist among some lesbians. Indeed, aside from their sexual preference for women, lesbians are no different from any other group. Like their heterosexual peers, lesbians who grow up in violent homes learn that battering is an acceptable form of behavior.

Forced to contend with prejudices against their race, gender and sexuality, lesbians of African descent bear additional burdens that can create strains in their intimate relationships. According to research conducted recently by University of California at Los Angeles psychologists Susan Cochran and Vickie Mays, a homosexual or bisexual Black woman suffers more depressive distress, including suicidal thoughts, than a gay Black man infected with

HIV.[1]

Their findings were based on levels of depressive distress measured through such indicators as blues, loneliness, fears, physical symptoms, relationship problems and frequency of suicidal thoughts.

Sylvia Rhue, a Los Angeles clinical social worker described the "triple whammy" of racism, sexism and homophobia experienced by Black lesbians this way:

> It's not because we're lesbian and Black that we have higher levels of psychiatric dysfunction, but because we have so many things put upon us by being Black and lesbian. Let's look at the economic factors that cause stress and depression. If you're female, you statistically make less than a man. If you're Black, you make statistically less than white people. If you're gay, you can be fired at any second and potentially have fewer opportunities if you're out of the closet.

Research conducted by Rhue shows that thirty-three percent of Black lesbians also face the stresses of being mothers. And all Black gays and lesbians are subject to disapproval and rejection from the most influential institution in the African-American community — the Black church.

Among Blacks, homosexuality has historically been viewed as an "abnormal" lifestyle that undermines the strength and power of the race. This attitude is based on the erroneous assumption that gays and lesbians do not have children.

Moreover, the scripture-based teachings against homosexuality espoused in the traditional Black church make many Black lesbians feel that their relationships are sinful. Abused Black lesbians can come to believe that the violence they are suffering is "punishment" from God because they are intimate with women, not men.

One Woman's Story

All the factors just outlined conspired to keep Belinda, a forty-three-year-old administrator, in an abusive relationship with another Black women for more than two years. The mother of two pre-teen sons, Belinda agreed to let her lover move in with her shortly after their romance began. A relationship that first appeared loving and supportive soon turned sour when the woman immediately began to control Belinda and her boys.

Rationalizing her behavior by saying that she wanted to keep their home tidy, the woman insisted that Belinda's sons stay holed up in their room most of the time. She also got upset whenever Belinda's friends or family members came to visit. The woman claimed to be head over heels in love with Belinda and thus demanded that they devote all their time and energy to the relationship. Flattered by the attention, Belinda soon found herself completely isolated from friends, relatives and co-workers.

Promises

The relationship deteriorated as the couple argued about meals, money, outings and the supervision of Belinda's children. The shouting matches escalated into physical fights. During one such altercation, Belinda shoved her lover while attempting to flee the room. Her lover fell to the floor, breaking her arm.

In the aftermath of each fight, the woman would express remorse and promise not to abuse Belinda again. She would be kind to the boys and bring them special treats. She would also buy Belinda gifts and cook her favorite meals and their strained sex life would improve.

It was during these "honeymoon phases" that Belinda felt nurtured by her lover and confident that the relationship would flourish. She said:

> There would be times when she'd be really nice to me. I'd come home and the house would be really clean and the boys seemed happy. I would relish the good times when she was feeling okay and the relationship seemed to be working. But then it would go back to being bad.

As with all batterers mired in the cycle of domestic violence, Belinda's partner made a promise she could not keep.

Paralysis

Belinda recalled another upsetting incident during which she feared her lover might strike her. She said she had invited a few friends to their home to celebrate her partner's birthday. Incensed that one of the guests had inadvertently put her foot up on the coffee table, Belinda's lover blamed her for the guest's behavior and began to berate her in front of the group.

"She started banging plates around and screaming at me to hurry up and cut the cake because she wanted people out of the house," Belinda said. "I was so embarrassed. I just asked people to leave."

Paralyzed by fear and ashamed to tell anyone about the mayhem in her life, Belinda tried desperately to "keep the lid on" her partner. She admonished her sons to behave and deferred to the woman's every request, all to no avail. Finally, in desperation, Belinda called an abused women's hotline and got information about obtaining a restraining order. But her shame about the relationship prevented her from following through. She believed, as her lover had told her, that she would be "laughed out of court" if she brought a domestic violence complaint against another woman. Throughout the ordeal, Belinda never once considered phoning the police for help.

At Belinda's insistence, her lover eventually moved out. In the wake of her departure, the woman ransacked Belinda's apartment and splattered paint all over her car. For more than a year after the breakup, Belinda received menacing phone calls from the woman. She lived in terror that her ex-lover would show up at her job and kill her, as the woman had threatened to do.

Scar Tissue

Nearly five years after her last contact with the woman, Belinda still carries the pain of the relationship. As part of her recovery process, Belinda started individual counseling and group therapy and made a decision to return to school.

Reflecting on her years in an abusive relationship, Belinda says:

> When I look back at the insanity of it all now, I know that I stayed because of my self-esteem. The fact that I didn't have any. It was the kind of relationship my mother had with my father. I saw my mother just stay and put up with the abuse, so that's what I learned.
>
> I was also ashamed to let anybody know what was happening in my house. I was ashamed about what I was putting my kids through. I felt really guilty. I blamed myself for getting involved with a woman who mistreated me. It was like I deserved it. It was my punishment for being a dyke.

Fran Staton, the Berkeley therapist, says that, as with abused heterosexual women, it is common for battered lesbians to feel responsible for the abuse they suffer. Fully aware of the powerlessness and invisibility that lesbians experience in most arenas of their lives, abused Black lesbians can be more willing to defer to their partners as a means of compensating for the slights their lovers suffer in the outside world.

Notes a Black woman involved with a prominent, but still struggling, Black lesbian singer: "My lover is more talented than most of her white lesbian peers. Sometimes she takes out her frustrations on me. It hurts, but I understand it."

Like their heterosexual counterparts, abusive Black lesbian relationships give rise to injury, alienation and mistrust. And children reared in violent lesbian households suffer damaging long-term effects.

Today in his early twenties, Belinda's youngest son says his childhood years were marred by the abusive acts he witnessed between his mother and her partner:

> They used to fight all the time. I mean every day there would

> be an argument about something. I was just a nine-year-old kid trying to play with my toys and read my comic books in peace. It was confusing. I didn't know what the hell was going on.
>
> Just the other day I was joking around with my girlfriend. I was trying to get my point across. I didn't hit her or push her or nothing. I gave her a little nudge. She called me "Ike Turner." She said I was playing too rough. I was shocked. I didn't realize it. I don't want to end up being violent. So I'm going to watch myself with that. I don't want to end up doing the same stuff I saw as a kid. I don't want to be a brute.

Battered lesbians can experience a variety of long-term problems including depression, anxiety, eating disorders, sexual dysfunction and substance abuse. Often unable to talk about the abuse because of anti-gay bias, many suffer in isolation and shame. Some avoid future intimate relationships out of a fear of being violated again.

Belinda attributes the failure of a subsequent relationship, in part, to the physical and emotional pain she endured with her abusive partner:

> I didn't give the woman a chance. There was no way, shape or form that I was ever going to be abused again so I was intolerant of a lot of stuff with this woman. I didn't cut her any slack. Right now, I'd love to be in a relationship, but I'm scared at the same time. I have a lot of mistrust.

Getting Help

Lesbians working to get out of an abusive relationship have the same options available to heterosexual women. However, because of homophobia or a lack of sensitivity to the issues involved in same-sex violence, lesbians can encounter problems exercising those options and getting access to already limited services.

The most important step a battered lesbian can take is to tell someone about the abuse. Although you may have concerns about revealing your sexual identity, or shame about being mistreated by another woman, remember that your safety depends on breaking the conspiracy of silence about your abuse.

Domestic violence continues, in part, because batterers are not held accountable for their actions. They are often in denial about their behavior and will claim the violence is their partner's fault. By sharing your experiences with a friend, family member or helping professional you develop resources that can provide intervention in your abuse.

The Police

The commonly held view of domestic violence is gendered: men batter, women are battered. Because of this view, police have a tendency to minimize abuse in gay/lesbian relationships.

They may be reluctant to write up an incident report because the complainants are women. They may suggest that lesbianism is the problem rather than any violent or criminal act.

However, battered women's advocates stress adamantly that fear of a homophobic legal system should not keep lesbians who are in imminent danger from calling the police. Assault, perpetrated by *any* person against *any* person is against the law in *every* state in the country.

If the situation is dangerous, call the police. There's no guarantee that "Officer Do Right" will come to help, but some help in an emergency is better than nothing.

The Criminal Justice System

The statutory definition of domestic violence varies from state to state. Although a lesbian battered anywhere by her partner has a right to get help from police, lesbians may have difficulty obtaining access to such legal tools as a temporary restraining order. A legal advocate from a battered women's shelter, a gay/lesbian law organization or service agency is your best resource for finding out how to get a restraining order (See Resources).

Stanford Law School student Adele M. Morrison is an African-American woman who has conducted research on lesbian battering. She offers the following words for Black lesbians in abusive relationships to consider:

> In a few instances, it may simplify legal proceedings to approach the particular "incident" that brings a battered lesbian to the legal system as an assault. Because of homophobia, the system might be more likely to offer some remedy if the woman does not include the history of abuse or the truth about her relationship (i.e., that the perpetrator is her lover or ex-lover) as part of her case.
>
> However, this can be a risky tactic, especially when the issue is a battered lesbian who has killed her partner. The lover/partner relationship, which is an aspect of the "battered women's syndrome," (a theory utilized to successfully defend some women), can excuse or justify the action taken. When the true nature of the relationship is not introduced, then the "battered women's syndrome" can not be used as a mitigating factor or as evidence for a self-defense claim.[2]

Shelters and Counseling

To date, shelters specifically for battered lesbians do not exist. Because the lesbian community, for the most part, has not admitted that the problem exists, there is a nationwide dearth of services for lesbian and bisexual women who have been battered by other women.

The shelters and counseling services available to battered heterosexual women are available to lesbians in abusive relationships; however, a battered lesbian may encounter service providers who are unfamiliar with the issues involved in same-sex domestic violence.

You can minimize the possibility that you will be "harmed" again by an insensitive police officer, therapist, shelter worker or legal advocate by asking a trusted friend or family member to assist you in your efforts to get help. This means, as stated previously, you must tell someone about your abuse. As long as discussions about woman-to-woman domestic violence are silenced, the community cannot support the survivors or confront the batterers, and nothing will change.

Subject to racism, sexism and homophobia, Black lesbians in abusive relationships, clearly, have additional obstacles to face. But by focusing on your needs and your right to a loving partner, you can transform those obstacles into tools of empowerment.

As Belinda says:

> First of all, do not believe that the person is going to change. No matter what you do, she's not going to change. Don't keep it to yourself. Tell somebody you are being abused and try to get help. If you're a battered lesbian, you might think there's no way out. But there is. I'm living proof.

CHAPTER NINE

A Higher Love

You might wonder if it is really possible to learn to nurture yourself and make changes that will free you from an abusive relationship. As Chaka Khan sings, "As strange as it seems, we make our own dreams come true."

To begin the process of ending the violence in your life, it is essential that you tell someone you are being abused. It is impossible to change your situation or for others to help you if you do not admit there is something wrong in your household. As difficult as it may be to accept that your partner is abusing you, you must stop denying or minimizing the reality of your situation. Of course, it is easy to deny painful or unpleasant things if you think you are the cause of them. This is a defense mechanism all humans have. Hopefully, information you have read in this book thus far has helped you understand that you are not responsible for your partner's abusive behavior. As Elaine said, "On the 4th of July when he came home and jumped on me because the store ran out of charcoal, I finally accepted that this was really his problem and not my fault. I wasn't going to get beat up every time he wanted to barbecue."

Your partner must want to change his behavior. He must believe, contrary to what he's learned in society, that he does not have the right to strike you or anyone else because he's a man. He must learn to work out his frustrations about living in a racist society in healthy, productive ways — not by taking his anguish out on you. These may sound like revolutionary suggestions in a society where all young boys are taught to fight back and violence is viewed by many as an acceptable way of dealing with the often brutal injustices of racism. Perhaps it is through such "radical" thoughts and social changes that our tolerance of all forms of violence in American society will end.

Meanwhile, you can put an end to your personal abuse by learning to love yourself in all your dimensions as a Black woman. This does not mean you have to abandon your relationship or betray the Black race. You can be supportive and understanding of your partner while acknowledging that it is his responsibility to change his abusive behavior. You might discuss setting up a time schedule by which he will enroll in counseling or job training programs to prove he is sincere about changing his life. This does not mean that you are domineering, simply that you believe you deserve a caring, non-abusive relationship.

Taking such action will help rid you of many of the negative stereotypes you have internalized both within and outside of the relationship. The destructive images and actions are all around you — Black women murdered, Black women raped, "fat, lazy and always pregnant" Black women in welfare lines. These images are pervasive in our society. They filter in and affect us, no matter how much Black pride or self-esteem we tell ourselves we have.

Learn to recognize your own self-hatred. Take an honest assessment of what you do and do not like about yourself, and evaluate how much of your feelings are based on white beauty standards or symbols of success. How often do you greet other African-American women you might pass on the street? Do you bypass Blacks in stores, banks or other professional settings because you assume we are less competent in our jobs than whites? Do you seek out the Black women in your community who appear to be improving their lives, or do you assume they think they're "better" than you? Have you ever considered that other African-American women might really value having you as a friend? Your honest answers to these questions can give you an indication of what you really think about yourself and other Black women. Remember the emotional scars in all of us run deep. They go back as far as our history in this country, and none of us will recover from the damage overnight. But we cannot begin to overcome our insecurities or self-hatred until we take an honest look at why these feelings exist.

It is not selfish to nurture yourself as you have nurtured so many others. Go back to school, take a vacation, exercise, pursue the jobs you are really interested in and believe you are qualified to do. So much of our Black beauty and abilities have been disguised by poverty, nutritional deficiencies, and excessive physical and emotional stress. You can begin to overcome some of these patterns if you start taking some steps toward a more healthy life as Roz, one abused African-American woman, did:

> I'm not the kind of woman who is ever going to exercise on a regular basis. But I've always wanted to be more physically active. So I decided I'd help my son with his paper route one day a week. I go out with him and help deliver the papers. I enjoy walking and meeting the people in the neighborhood. My son likes it too because he says having me with him makes it easier to collect the money.

Changing your patterns and your relationship will involve pain, fear and lots of hard work. Some days you may feel lonely, depressed, angry and overwhelmed by it all. You may get sick of calling the police, listening to attorneys or spilling your heart out to a therapist and wondering if any of it is helping at all. You may be tempted to just give up and live with things the way they are.

The police, attorneys, counselors, shelter workers, friends, relatives, etc., are very important resources who can be supportive and help you change the direction of your life. However, none of them have the absolute power to stop your partner from abusing you. Not one of them can do more for you than you can do for yourself, by taking the steps that will make you really believe you deserve a loving, non-abusive relationship.

Like Black poet M. Eliza Hamilton, whose poem closes this book, turn toward yourself and face every word and deed that has ever hurt you. You'll probably feel pain and shed many tears. But you'll also discover that you can cry and the world will not fall apart. You'll find that you are still a loving, caring, gifted, valuable, unique and beautiful Black woman. You are a Black woman who deserves to be loved and respected by your partner, as well as the rest of society.

Turning to Face Home

The journey
of Fear
and Denial

ends here

at the center
of the Self
I have uprooted

to root again

in this space
gutted and razed

fists will never be forgotten

but
once more

there is rain
and air
for roots
to take hold
of me

Me

being born
every minute

every moment
roots delving
deeper

in my Self

this journey
of Fear
and Denial

ends here.

— M. Eliza Hamilton

Notes

Introduction

1. Uniform Crime Reports, Washington, D.C.: U.S. Department of Justice, 1983-1989.
2. "Female Victims of Violent Crime," Washington, D.C.: U.S. Department of Justice, 1991.
3. Byllye Y. Avery, "Breathing Life Into Ourselves: The Evolution of the Black Women's Health Project," *Sojourner*, Volume XIV, Number 5, January 1989.
4. Jose Torres, *Fire and Fear: The Inside Story of Mike Tyson* (New York: Warner Books, 1989), p. 132.
5. Robin Givens, "So How Do You Like Me Now?," *Playboy*, September 1994, pages 120-130.
6. *New York Times*, August 15, 1993, p. 1.
7. *Ibid.*, p. 1.

Chapter One

1. Evelyn Reed, *Women's Evolution* (New York: Pathfinder Press, 1975), p. 96.
2. Testimony by Senator Joseph R. Biden, Jr., The Violence Against Women Act, January 21, 1993, p. 3.
3. Federal Bureau of Investigation, "Crime in the United States," Uniform Crime Reports for the United States 1989, August 1990, p. 12.
4. Lenore Walker, *The Battered Woman* (New York: Harper & Row, 1979), p. 55-70.

Chapter Two

1. Zora Neale Hurston, "How It Feels to Be Colored Me," in *I Love Myself When I Am Laughing* (Old Westbury: The Feminist Press, 1978), p. 153.
2. Barbara Smith, introduction to *Home Girls* (New York: Kitchen Table Press, 1983), pp. xxxiv-xxxv.
3. Gail Garfield, "Exposing the Silence: Violence As Experienced In the Lives of African-American Women," unpublished paper, October 1991.
4. Alice Walker, "The Civil Rights Movement: What Good Was It?" in *In Search of Our Mother's Gardens* (New York: Harcourt Brace Jovanovich, 1983), p. 123.
5. Alice Walker, *The Third Life of Grange Copeland* (New York: Harcourt Brace Jovanovich, 1970), p. 55.
6. Marital Status and Living Arrangements, U.S. Census Bureau Report, July 1994.

7. *The Speaking Profits Us: Violence in the Lives of Women of Color,* monograph by the Center for the Prevention of Sexual and Domestic Violence, Seattle, Washington, 1986, p. 4.
8. *Seattle Times,* June 15, 1985.

Chapter Three

1. Beth Richie-Bush, "Facing Contradictions: Challenge for Black Feminists," *Aegis,* no. 37, 1983.
2. Bureau of Justice Statistics, "Report to the Nation, 2nd edition," Washington, D.C.: U.S. Department of Justice, 1988, p. 3.

Chapter Seven

1. Eleanor Johnson, "Reflections: On Black Feminist Therapy," in *Conditions Five: The Black Women's Issue,* 1979, p. 113.

Chapter Eight

1. Susan Cochran and Vicki Mays, "Depressive Distress Among Homosexually Active African American Men and Women," *American Journal of Psychiatry,* April 1994, pages 524-529.
2. Written memo to author, August 1994.

Suggested Reading and Resources

Information and support are vital for battered women. The following selected list can be useful to abused African-American women and those working to assist them.

BOOKS

Angelou, Maya. *I Know Why The Caged Bird Sings.* New York: Random House, 1970.

Bolton, Ruthie. *Gal.* New York: Harcourt, 1994.

Boyd, Julia. *In The Company of My Sisters: Black Women and Self-Esteem.* New York: Dutton, 1993.

Ferrato, Donna. *Living With the Enemy.* New York: Aperture, 1988.

Fortune, Marie and Hormann, Denise. *Family Violence: A Workshop Manual for Clergy and Other Service Providers.* Seattle: The Center for the Prevention of Sexual and Domestic Violence, 1980.

Gaines, Patrice. *Laughing In The Dark.* New York: Crown, 1994.

Golden, Marita, ed. *Wild Women Don't Wear No Blues: Black Women Writers on Love, Men and Sex.* New York: Doubleday, 1993.

Gomez, Jewelle. *Forty-Three Septembers.* Ithaca, NY: Firebrand, 1993.

hooks, bell. *Sisters Of The Yam: Black Women and Self-Recovery.* Boston: South End Press, 1993.

Jones, Ann. *Next Time, She'll Be Dead: Battering and How to Stop It.* Boston: Beacon, 1994.

Lee, Helen Elaine. *The Serpent's Gift.* New York: Atheneum, 1994.

Lobel, Kerry, ed. *Naming the Violence: Speaking Out About Lesbian Battering.* Seattle: Seal Press, 1986.

McMillan, Terri. *Disappearing Acts.* New York: Viking, 1989.

McMillan, Terri. *Waiting to Exhale.* New York: Viking, 1992.

Morrison, Toni. *Beloved.* New York: Plume, 1987.

Morrison, Toni. *The Bluest Eye.* New York: Knopf, 1970.

Morrison. Toni. *Sula.* New York: Knopf, 1973

Naylor, Gloria. *The Women of Brewster Place.* New York: Viking, 1983.

Nelson, Jill. *Volunteer Slavery: My Authentic Negro Experience.* Chicago: Noble, 1993.

NiCarthy, Ginny. *Getting Free: A Handbook for Women in Abusive Relationships.* Seattle: Seal Press, 1982.

NiCarthy, Ginny, Merriam, Karen and Coffman, Sandra. *Talking It Out: A Guide to Groups for Abused Women.* Seattle: Seal Press, 1985.

Paris, Susan. *Mommy and Daddy Are Fighting: A Book for Children About Domestic Violence.* Seattle: Seal Press, 1985.

Shange, Ntozake. *For Colored Girls Who Have Considered Suicide When the Rainbow Is Enuf.* New York: Macmillan, 1977.

Shange, Ntozake. *Liliane: Resurrection of the Daughter.* New York: St. Martin's Press, 1994.

Sinclair, April. *Coffee Will Make You Black.* New York: Hyperion, 1994.

Villarosa, Linda, ed. *Body and Soul: The Black Women's Guide to Physical Health and Emotional Well-Being.* New York: HarperCollins, 1994.

Walker, Alice. *The Color Purple.* New York: Harcourt, 1982.

Walker, Alice. *The Third Life of Grange Copeland.* New York: Harcourt, 1970.

White, Evelyn C., ed. *The Black Women's Health Book: Speaking For Ourselves.* Seattle: Seal Press, 1994.

Wilson, Melba. *Crossing The Boundary: Black Women Survive Incest.* Seattle: Seal Press, 1994.

VIDEOS

What's Love Got to Do With It?: The Triumphant True-Life Story of Tina Turner (1993), directed by Brian Gibson, Touchstone Pictures. Available at video outlets.

Defending Our Lives (1993), produced by Margaret Lazarus, Renner Wunderlich and Stacy Kabat. Cambridge Documentary Films, P.O. Box 385, Cambridge, Massachusetts 02139.

ORGANIZATIONS

Battered Women's Justice Project
206 West Fourth Street
Duluth, Minnesota 55806
(800) 903-0111
Addresses the criminal and civil justice systems, responds to violence and battered women's self-defense.

A Circle of Sisters: Conscious Connections
c/o Hafeezah Basir
The Unlimited Self
405 West 147th Street
New York, New York 10031
A national directory of sister support groups.

Family Violence Prevention Fund Health Resource Center
383 Rhode Island Street, Suite 304
San Francisco, California 94103
(800) 313-1310
Provides general information packets to strengthen the health care response to domestic violence and a library to support health-care based domestic violence training.

The National Black Women's Health Project
1237 Abernathy Boulevard
Atlanta, Georgia 30310
(800) 275-2947
Provides self-help groups and health advocacy for African-American women.

The National Center for Lesbian Rights
870 Market Street, Suite 570
San Francisco, California 94102
(415) 392-6257
Provides legal assistance for lesbians.

The National Coalition Against Domestic Violence
P.O. Box 18749
Denver, Colorado 80218
(303) 839-1852
Provides information on support groups, advocacy agencies, and resources on domestic violence.

National Resource Center on Domestic Violence
6400 Flank Drive, Suite 1300
Harrisburg, Pennsylvania 17112
(800) 537-2238
Provides comprehensive ways to enhance community responses to domestic violence.

The Center for the Prevention of Sexual and Domestic Violence
1914 N. 34th Street, Suite 105
Seattle, Washington 98103
(206) 634-1903
Provides materials and education about abuse within the context of religious communities.

Community United Against Violence
973 Market Street, Suite 500
San Francisco, California 94103
(415) 777-5500
Addresses anti-gay violence and provides support for gays and lesbians in abusive relationships.

Resource Center on Child Custody and Child Protection
P.O. Box 8970
Reno, Nevada 89507
(800) 527-3223
Provides materials, expert consultation, technical assistance and legal research related to child protection and custody within the context of domestic violence.

Women of Color Resource Center
2288 Fulton Street, Suite 103
Berkeley, California 94704
(510) 848-9272
Publishes a national directory of Women of Color Organizations and Projects.

Acknowledgments

I remain indebted to the friends and colleagues who assisted me with the completion of the first edition of this book. Through invaluable suggestions and support, they each made a contribution to the empowerment of abused African-American women.

In addition, I now offer my heartfelt thanks to Diane Bryant, Derrick Hammond, Jessica Holter, Chana Kai Lee, Elaine Lee and Fran Staton.

The women of Seal Press, especially my editor Faith Conlon, recognized the importance of publishing an expanded edition of *Chain Chain Change.* Thanks for your continued commitment to the struggle.

The dozens of abused Black women who shared their experiences with me deserve special recognition. Many thanks for letting me bear witness to your vulnerabilities and strengths.

For exquisite words that affirm the journey and transformation of Black women, I thank poets Nikky Finney and M. Eliza Hamilton.

Blessings to Stanford Law School student Adele M. Morrison and San Francisco Chronicle librarian Kathleen Rhodes for vital research.

Jane Gottesman, my assistant and cherished writer friend, transcribed tapes, tracked down reference works, delivered chicken soup and took me to Cirque du Soleil. She brought much needed light and laughter to this project.

I am forever grateful to Mona Vold, whose love has comforted me in this life and many others.

Liz Hafalia

Evelyn C. White is the editor of *The Black Women's Health Book*, the co-author of the photography book, *The African Americans,* and is currently writing the autobiography of Alice Walker. She lectures widely on Black women's physical and emotional health, and her writing has appeared in numerous publications, including *Essence*, *Smithsonian* and *The Wall Street Journal.* She lives in Oakland, California.

Selected Titles from Seal Press

THE BLACK WOMEN'S HEALTH BOOK: *Speaking for Ourselves*, expanded second edition, edited by Evelyn C. White. $16.95, 1-878067-40-0. More than fifty Black women write about the health issues that affect them and the well-being of their families and communities. Contributors include Faye Wattleton, Byllye Y. Avery, Alice Walker, Angela Y. Davis, Zora Neale Hurston, Audre Lorde, Lucille Clifton, bell hooks and Toni Morrison.

CROSSING THE BOUNDARY: *Black Women Survive Incest* by Melba Wilson. $12.95, 1-878067-42-7. Focusing on the dynamics of sex and sexual oppression as they intersect with gender, class and race, Wilson includes the voices of survivors, a discussion of the role of professionals and an exploration of works by Maya Angelou, Alice Walker, Buchi Emecheta and other Black women writers.

GETTING FREE: *You Can End Abuse and Take Back Your Life* by Ginny NiCarthy. $12.95, 1-878067-92-3. The most important self-help resource book of the domestic violence movement. Also Available on Audiocassette: GETTING FREE: *Are You Abused? (And What to Do About It)* narrated by Ginny NiCarthy, 60 minutes. $10.95, 0-931188-84-9.

YOU CAN BE FREE: *An Easy-to-Read Handbook for Abused Women* by Ginny NiCarthy and Sue Davidson. $10.95, 0-931188-68-7. A simplified version of *Getting Free*, written in a straightforward style for women with basic reading skills and for women in crisis.

A WOMAN LIKE YOU: *The Face of Domestic Violence,* interviews and photographs by Vera Anderson. $16.00, 1-878067-07-9. A profoundly inspiring photo-essay book about women who left abusive relationships and rebuilt their lives. Features portraits of women in their new lives and their stories as told in their own words.

MOMMY AND DADDY ARE FIGHTING: *A Book for Children About Family Violence* by Susan Paris. $8.95, 0-931188-33-4. Written from a child's perspective, this gentle and supportive illustrated book tells about the confusing experience of living in a violent home.

NAMING THE VIOLENCE: *Speaking Out Against Lesbian Battering* edited by Kerry Lobel. $12.95, 0-931188-42-3. This groundbreaking anthology deals with the problem of physical and emotional abuse in lesbian relationships.

IN LOVE AND IN DANGER: *A Teen's Guide to Breaking Free of Abusive Relationships* by Barrie Levy. $8.95, 1-878067-26-5. An important, straightforward book for teens caught in abusive dating relationships.

DATING VIOLENCE: *Young Women in Danger* edited by Barrie Levy. $16.95, 1-878067-03-6. Both a call for action and a tool for change, this book is the first comprehensive resource for teens in sexually, emotionally or physically abusive relationships.

TALKING IT OUT: *A Guide to Groups for Abused Women* by Ginny NiCarthy, Karen Merriam and Sandra Coffman. $12.95, 0-931188-24-5. An informative and comprehensive handbook for counselors, mental health workers, and shelter or community activists on starting and sustaining a group for abused women.

MEJOR SOLA QUE MAL ACOMPAÑADA: *For the Latina in an Abusive Relationship/Para la Mujer Golpeada* by Myrna M. Zambrano. $12.95, 0-931188-26-1. A bilingual handbook in Spanish and English offering support, helpful advice, understanding and practical information on many issues and questions about abusive relationships.

A COMMUNITY SECRET: *For the Filipina in an Abusive Relationship* by Jacqueline R. Agtuca, in collaboration with The Asian Women's Shelter. $5.95, 1-878067-44-3. In easy-to-read English, three Filipinas tell their stories. Topics include why men batter, what to do about the children, immigration and the law, and resources for ending abuse.

YOU DON'T HAVE TO TAKE IT!: *A Woman's Guide to Confronting Emotional Abuse at Work* by Ginny NiCarthy, Naomi Gottlieb and Sandra Coffman. $14.95, 1-878067-35-4. This comprehensive guide provides practical advice and exercises to help women recognize abusive situations and respond with constructive action, including assertive confrontation and workplace organizing.

ORDERING INFORMATION: If you are unable to obtain a Seal Press title from a bookstore, please order from us directly. Enclose payment with your order and 16.5% of the book total for shipping and handling. Washington residents should add 8.6% sales tax. Checks, MasterCard and Visa accepted. If ordering with a credit card, please include your name as it appears on the card, the expiration date and your signature. Send to: Orders Dept., Seal Press, 3131 Western Avenue, Suite 410, Seattle, Washington 98121. 1-800-754-0271 orders only. Visit our website at www.sealpress.com and email us at sealpress@sealpress.com.

Printed in the United States
963700002B